John Biedemann

John Biedemann

Giants of Invention

Giants of Invention

By EDGAR THARP

ILLUSTRATED BY FRANK VAUGHAN

PUBLISHERS

Grosset & Dunlap

NEW YORK

CONTENTS

[5]

THE UNKNOWN GIANTS

WE DO NOT KNOW who the first inventor was, or, for that matter, what he invented. But whatever it was, it helped to determine the subsequent progress man has made, and is probably one of the basic tools of life today, although it was invented some 100,000 years ago. Many of the fundamental inventions which we take for granted today — the plow, the wheel, hand tools — were given to us by these unknown inventors of ancient times. A few of the inventions attributed to the unknowns are listed below:

abacus	lock
axe	money
boat	needle
bow and arrow	oar
brake	plow
cart	potter's wheel
chain	pottery
chisel	pulley
clothing	raft
cogwheel	rope
cooking	rudder
digging stick	sail
fire	saw
hammer	screw
harness	shovel
hinge	sled
hoe	sling
hour glass	spinning
irrigation systems	weaving
knife	wedge
lamp	wheel
lever	yoke

A controlled fire was among the earliest of inventions. The inventor was one of our prehistoric ancestors who probably first learned of fire when lightning started a forest fire near his cave. He learned that this strange, flickering flame gave heat and light, and later that it could be used to cook food. It was probably by chance that he learned how to make this strange magic himself. One theory is that he was making a new stone axe by chipping one rock against another when a spark from the chipping ignited some dry leaves nearby. But however fire was first discovered, this man is probably the greatest inventor of all time; for in one fell swoop he gave us light, heat, and the means to cook our food.

Hand tools were also among the early inventions. Stone tools and weapons were in use some 100,000 years ago during the early Stone Age. These were crude knives and scrapers and axes which were simply held in the hand when used. Like later inventors, some Stone Age tinker decided to improve on these tools and added a handle to the knife and axe and later learned to make spears and arrows with stone heads.

Like all inventors, these unknowns drew freely on the experience and inventions of others, and as man's body of knowledge increased, so did his inventiveness. The Bronze Age supplanted the Stone Age and tools became sharper and harder and easier to fashion. Then some one invented iron and these bronze and copper tools were outmoded.

Some 10,000 years ago prehistoric man began

to cultivate plants for food. This gave rise to the digging stick and the hoe and the sickle for reaping. Sometime around 3,000 B.C., after animals had been domesticated, an Egyptian invented the plow to make the farmer's lot easier. This period gave us many of our basic tools and instruments, for it was around 3,000 B.C. that inventors produced the sail to power boats, the wheel, the water wheel, the potter's wheel, the wedge, lever, gears, screws, the pulley, and others.

The inventions of these unknown giants came about much like those that followed in later times. They were motivated by necessity or by sheer curiosity and some came about simply by chance; but whatever the reason, their contributions to man's progress is as unmeasured as their names are unknown.

Before Technology

ARCHIMEDES

(287 B.C.–212 B.C.)

The Beginnings of Technology

MAN had few mechanical devices to make his work easier when Archimedes was born in 287 B.C. in the Greek city-state of Syracuse on the island of Sicily. The wheel, the sail for ships, the inclined plane, the lever, and a few other basic tools were all man had to work with. Archimedes' mechanical inventions were not his greatest contribution to mankind, but they are memorable because they are perhaps the first inventions that can actually be attributed to an inventor.

Although the Greek scientist's contributions in mathematics and physics are authenticated by the remarkable collection of written works he left behind, his mechanical inventions are more a product of legend than of recorded history. However, it is generally conceded that he invented the Archimedean screw, the compound pulley, the endless screw, and a number of machines of war such as the catapult.

The Archimedean screw is believed to have been invented about 250 B.C. while Archimedes was living in Alexandria, Egypt. It was designed primarily to raise water from the Nile River to irrigate fields above the water level of the river. The device consists of a pipe twisted in a spiral form around a central axis. The screw is placed at an angle, with the lower end in the water. When the screw is made to revolve, the water is raised from bend to bend in the spiral pipe until it flows out at the top.

Little is known of the other mechanical inventions of Archimedes, but an interesting story is generally told of his discovery of the "Archimedean Principle," a law in physics which is used in determining specific gravity. The king of Syracuse, Hiero II, asked Archimedes to determine whether a new crown made for him was pure gold, or whether the goldsmith had cheated him and alloyed it with silver. While pondering the problem in the bathtub, Archimedes noticed that the amount of water that flowed over the side of the tub when he got in was equal to the amount in which his body was immersed. He rushed naked from the bath house shouting "Eureka" (Greek for "I have found it."). He tested the crown by his new principle and found that the goldsmith had cheated Hiero. The discovery of the principle that a solid immersed in a liquid displaces an amount of liquid equal to its weight was the first step in the founding of the science of hydrostatics.

In the Greek tradition, Archimedes regarded

himself as a philosopher and mathematician, which, indeed, he was. He scorned the practical inventions he made as mere amusements, for this was not yet an age of technology, and science consisted of philosophical and mathematical speculation.

Even so, tradition has it that — just as today — his greatest inventions were turned to the uses of war. It is related that he built a huge burning glass that set fire to the Roman fleet besieging his home city, but this seems doubtful.

In any case, this peaceful philosopher died by the sword. A Roman soldier found him drawing a mathematical figure on the sand and slew him on the spot. This despite the fact that the Roman general Marcellus, aware of the man's greatness, had ordered his troops to leave Archimedes and his home unharmed.

Even as victory was his, the Roman general mourned the death of one of the greatest thinkers of the classical world. He directed that Archimedes be buried with honors, and on his tomb was placed a sphere surrounded by a cylinder, because the philosopher had regarded as his greatest achievement the discovery of the relation between a sphere and cylinder.

JOHANN GUTENBERG

(1400–1468)

Printing Awakens Man's Mind

THE IDEA OF printing from movable type was born one day when a boy watched a jeweler make a sand mold for a metal brooch in order to cast a duplicate of the original brooch. Young Johann Gutenberg already had conceived the idea of printing from movable type, but the wooden blocks on which he carved the letters of the alphabet kept splitting when he tried to impress the letters on paper. From the jeweler he got the idea of casting his letters in metal. But it took many years of untold hardships and disappointments before the art of printing became an actuality.

Johann Gutenberg was born of a noble family in Mainz, Germany, about 1400. Little is known of his boyhood, but while in his teens he was apprenticed to learn the art of cutting and polishing precious stones. It was during this period that he became adept at using hand tools and in working with metals. Gutenberg finished his apprenticeship, but at the age of 30 was forced to flee the city of Mainz because of political persecution.

While still an apprentice, Johann had experimented with his idea of printing from movable type, hoping to perfect an easier method for producing books than the painstaking one of copying them by hand, the only method available at the time. When he left Mainz, he settled in Strasbourg, and obtained work as a jewel cutter. He continued his experiments, trying to find a practical way to mold his letters. He finally hit upon the idea of carving the face of the letters on a steel punch, and used this punch to form matrices (molds) for his letters. He now had the method of producing movable type, but lacked the financial backing to perfect his invention. He had formed a partnership in Strasbourg for this purpose, but his backers had become discouraged at the length of time it was taking the inventor to perfect the invention, and they withdrew their support.

Gutenberg returned to Mainz, where the political scene had become less stormy, and formed another partnership. He determined to print a Bible with his new type, but first he had to devise a press on which the book could be printed. This first printing press (1450) was modeled after the wine presses of the day. The form containing the type was placed on a platform above which a screw was attached to a crossbeam. A flat block of wood called a plate was attached to the screw. The type was inked and a piece of paper laid on top of the form. Then, by turning the screw, the plate was forced down onto the paper, causing the inked type to print.

Gutenberg's first Bible was printed in 1456. It contained 1282 pages and was bound in two volumes. But bad luck again plagued the inventor. His partner turned out to be little less than a greedy money lender. Aware of the potentialities of Gutenberg's type and press, he sued the inventor and was awarded all of his matrices, type, press, and the Bibles he had printed.

But despite the fact that he had been robbed of his invention, was penniless, and had reached the age of 56, Gutenberg was not discouraged. He sent to Strasbourg for the original type he had stored there, built another press, and by 1461 printed his second Bible. And during the last seven years of his life, the man who invented printing finally found security and recognition. The archbishop of Mainz, impressed by the Bibles that Gutenberg had printed, appointed him to his staff with a yearly pension.

The art of printing was fast spreading throughout Europe, and Johann Gutenberg was recognized as the master. Many young men came to Mainz to be taught this new art by the inventor. He even found time to print one more book before he died, the *Catholicon*, a Latin dictionary.

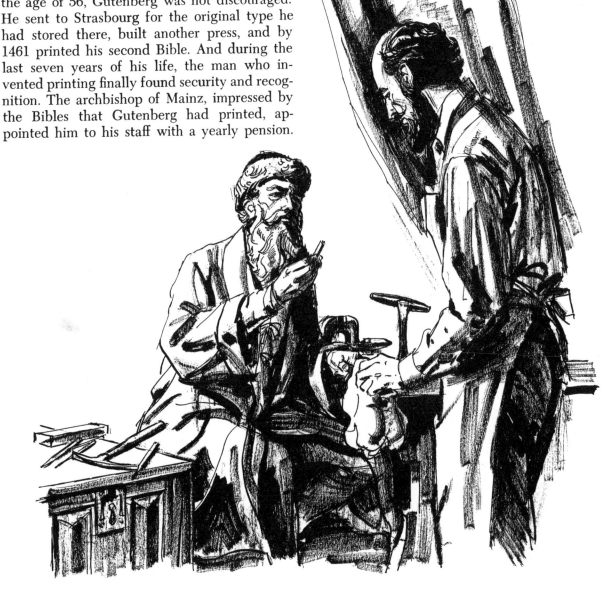

GALILEO GALILEI

(1564–1642)

Secrets of the Skies Unlocked

A NEW STAR appeared in the skies in 1604, and its appearance revolutionized the science of astronomy. The new star aroused the scientific curiosity of Galileo Galilei, then an instructor at the University of Padua in Italy, and he began to observe this new heavenly body. This interest in the stars led him, five years later, to the invention of the telescope.

Galileo's observance of a new star marked the beginning of his career as an active astronomer, but his interest in astronomy and in theoretical studies in the field had begun much earlier. He had read and studied the works of Aristotle and Ptolemy, who believed that the earth stood still and that the sun and planets revolved around it. This theory was generally held to be true for some 14 centuries, until in 1543 a Polish astronomer named Nicolaus Copernicus introduced a new theory that changed the thinking of the Western World. Copernicus, in his book *De Revolutionibus*, held that the earth was not a stationary body, but moved in orbit around the sun, as did the other planets. This new theory contradicted the theologian's literal interpretation of the Bible that man lived at the center of the universe, and was termed heretical by the Catholic Church. Galileo's acceptance of the Copernican Theory caused him much trouble in later life.

While teaching at Padua in 1609, Galileo learned of an eyeglass developed by Hans Lippershey which made distant objects visible to the eye. He immediately grasped the significance of Lippershey's crude telescope, and in a few days they invented the first practical refracting telescope. The first instrument he built was demonstrated publicly in August of 1609: it was a tube of sheet metal, 24″ long and about 3″ in diameter, with two lenses (convex and concave).

Turning his new invention to the sky later that year, his discoveries were as startling to the world in his day as was the launching of the first man in space some 350 years later. Galileo discovered that the planet Jupiter had at least 4 satellites; that the moon's surface is similar to that of the earth; and that the Milky Way is made up of thousands of stars.

Galileo published his findings in 1610 in a book called *The Starry Messenger*. The news of the telescope and the marvels it had revealed spread like wildfire in the scientific world. The inventor was hailed generally by friends and scientists, though there were those who doubted his claims.

But Galileo is not only known as a great astronomer who invented the telescope. He also excelled in the field of physics and mathematics, and was one of the fathers of the Scientific Revolution brought about by such men as Bacon, Newton, Descartes, and others. Among his other contributions to progress were the hydrostatic

balance for determining specific gravity; the thermometer; and a geometric and military compass (sector). In the field of physics he discovered the law of inertia, the law regarding the regularity of pendulums which led to the invention of the pendulum clock, and several other laws; he also established the fact that the velocity of falling bodies is the same regardless of differences in weight.

Galileo ended his days under house arrest. In 1632 he published his *Dialogue Concerning the two chief World Systems*, in which he defended Copernicus' theory of the universe. He was accused of heresy by the Inquisition and was forced to recant. Galileo's book was banned and he was more or less kept under house arrest until he died in 1642.

ANTONY VAN LEEUWENHOEK

(1632-1723)

He Revealed a Hidden World

ANTONY VAN LEEUWENHOEK was a seventeenth century Dutch dry goods dealer. He was a suspicious, irritable, arrogant man who devoted more time and interest to his hobby than to his shopkeeping.

He seemed a queer fish indeed to the respectable burghers of that clean town with its neat canals and pretty windmills. He was born there in 1632, a time when the world was, as yet, scarcely aware of its own ignorance. And, speaking of ignorance, it must be admitted that Leeuwenhoek was no model of brilliance or genius. Yet he developed a device that may have saved more lives than any other invention.

As a matter of fact he was not much of a scholar at all. He somehow picked up a little mathematics, surveying, and a rudimentary knowledge of the physical sciences. He knew no Latin, which was the language of education in that day, and was hardly a master of the one language he could handle — his own Dutch, which was considered a lowly tongue by scholars of the time.

His father was a basketmaker and his mother came from a solid family of brewers, an occupation of considerable esteem in Holland to this day. Antony's training, however, consisted of learning the ins and outs of the drapery business, a trade by which he was to make his living.

At twenty-one Leeuwenhoek married and set up his own dry goods business in Delft. He had five children, four of whom died in infancy. The surviving child, a daughter named Maria, was his friend and helper till his death at the age of 91 in 1723.

Although Leeuwenhoek seems to have earned the loyalty and devotion of his daughter, he could hardly have been a model husband and parent. His dedication to his hobby could scarcely have left him enough time to spend with his family at all. And what was this "hobby?"

Magnifying glasses were known in Leeuwenhoek's day. A few primitive microscopes had already been constructed. Leeuwhenhoek was fascinated by the thought of seeing small objects enlarged many times. His fascination grew to a great passion which never left him. This simple man pursued his interest with the dogged determination of a fanatical man of action.

It was no easy matter in those days to go out and buy a good lens. Any lens he could have bought would not have satisfied him in any case. So Leeuwenhoek learned to grind his own lenses. He went to a fair at Delft and, after seeing a professional glass-blower at work, went home and taught himself to blow glass. He studied the arts of the goldsmiths and silversmiths and even learned how to extract his own metals from ores for the construction of his microscopes.

Can you think of what a formidable task this would be even today when the knowledge of this multitude of techniques is available to anyone who wishes to research it? In Antony van Leeuwenhoek's time all this was secret, to be ferreted out and discovered or rediscovered. It is almost certain that when he began this hobby which turned into such a great work of science and invention he had never even seen or heard of the little work others had done on the microscope.

But for this man who had a madness to peer into the smallest secrets of the world he lived in, the construction of the microscopes that had been known until that time would not have been good enough. He not only developed the microscope into a fine efficient instrument but also created the techniques of applying and using it. It is this application that is perhaps Leeuwenhoek's greatest contribution to humanity.

Picture this devoted crank spending innumerable hours of experiment in grinding and polishing minute lenses, in extracting metals over hot fires, in hammering, shaping, fitting parts to construct literally hundreds of microscopes, building many different models for different purposes.

Then can you imagine the staggering total of time he spent in looking through them; peering, gazing, studying, trying to find — what? What did this crochety inventor look at?

Under his microscopes he studied everything that came to his mind or his hand. From flowers to insect wings, everything went under his powerful eye. He studied the stinger of a bee, the eye of an ox or a fly. The hair of animals, the skin of man, the wood of trees, and seed of plants opened the secrets of their structure to him.

In pursuing these searches he discovered the great use of this great invention. Always, in his tireless, dogged way, he looked again, and compared again, over and over until he was certain of his results before setting down any of his findings.

After slaving in solitude for twenty years Leeuwenhoek brought his microscopes and his techniques of using them to the attention of the Royal Society of England which at that time was the foremost association of scientific investigators in the world. They invited him to tell them of his inventions and their results. As is the fate of so many discoverers and innovators in this world, our madman of the microscope was at first sneered at and laughed at — and finally accepted with homage.

And so we might well do him homage in memory of the day when he first placed a drop of clear rain water under his microscope. For on that day the "little beasts" — microbes — were discovered.

This great discovery, which came about through Leeuwenhoek and the invention of the microscope, is the cornerstone of a branch of medical science which opened mankind's brilliant battle against disease.

Antony van Leeuwenhoek's simple single-lens microscopes were followed by the more complex devices of multiple-lens construction. Today the electron microscope permits us to peer still further down in the world of infinite smallness. Tomorrow we shall get even closer to the core of the infinitesimal.

But always we shall be in debt to the microscope man of Delft who first pointed the way down into a world no one could see.

The Industrial Revolution

JAMES WATT

(1736–1819)

Steam Begins to Power Industry

IN THE latter part of the eighteenth century, water power was still the prime mover of the wheels of the infant industries of the world. During the same period the invention of new textile machinery in England gave rise to a demand for a greater source of power. Steam was the answer, and a Scotch instrument maker harnessed it successfully in 1765 by inventing a more practical steam engine.

James Watt did not invent the steam engine, but his improvements and new designs made it a practical and economical source of power. Long before Watt became interested in the subject, man had known some of the properties of steam. In 1690, Denis Papin, a Frenchman, had invented the first steam engine with a piston. Other pioneers in the field in England included Thomas Savery, who was the first to use a separate boiler in the steam engine, and Thomas Newcomen, who invented the "atmospheric" steam engine. These early machines were used for pumping water out of coal mines or supplying water to cities. However, it was not until James Watt entered the field that steam was successfully harnessed so as to turn industrial wheels.

Watt was born in Greenock, Scotland, on January 19, 1736. His father was an instrument maker, and it was in his father's shop that young James received his early training in mechanics.

At the age of eighteen he left his father's shop to seek further training in making scientific instruments. What he was seeking was not to be found in Glasgow, so he went to London. There he apprenticed himself to an instrument maker. Watt worked for a year at the trade, making quadrants, theodolites, an angle measurer, scales, compasses, and other such instruments. His talent was such that in a year he had completed a normal seven-year apprenticeship. He returned to Glasgow to set up shop for himself, but the guilds that controlled the trades there refused to let him work because he had not spent the required seven years as an apprentice.

Watt, then 21, could not see wasting another six years learning something he already knew. But what was he to do? His dilemma was solved when friends on the faculty of the University of Glasgow gave him a room in one of the buildings on the campus to work in. They also gave him his first contract for the repair of some of the university's scientific instruments.

The guild had no jurisdiction over the University's activities, and Watt's instrument business flourished. So did his friendship with the professors on the campus. He became interested in steam power in 1759 through discussions on the subject with his friend, Doctor Robinson. His first encounter with a steam engine was with a

Newcomen model the university used for teaching purposes. It was in bad condition, and Watt was given the task of overhauling it. He was not very successful, but from that time on the Scotch mechanic was obsessed with the idea of building a better steam engine.

The Newcomen or "atmospheric" steam engine was inefficient because it wasted much of its steam power. The boiler on this engine was separate from its combination cylinder-condenser, but steam was wasted when a jet of water was sprayed on the cylinder-condenser to condense the steam after the upward stroke, and thus create a vacuum, so that atmospheric pressure would force the piston down again. But this water spray cooled the cylinder encasing the piston, wasting steam to reheat the cylinder before the next upward stroke.

Watt wrestled with the problem until one Sunday afternoon in 1865; while taking a stroll on the Green in Glasgow, he hit upon the answer he needed for building a better steam engine. The combination cylinder-condenser must be separated so the cylinder could be kept constantly hot and the top of the cylinder sealed so that steam, rather than atmospheric pressure, made the engine work. The following day he built a scale model, and the principle of the condensing steam engine was born.

He entered into partnership with a Doctor Roebuck of Birmingham, and patented his first steam engine on January 5, 1769. Their business venture failed, however, and it was not until 1774, when Watt formed another partnership with Matthew Boulton of Birmingham, that his steam engine came into general use. In 1781 Watt patented his double-acting or rotary steam engine, a much improved version of the earlier machine.

The firm of Boulton and Watt prospered, providing English industry with a source of cheap and efficient power to run the mines and factories that were ever increasing as the Industrial Revolution gained momentum. Watt's engines were shipped all over the world; one of them powered the first practical steamboat ever built, Robert Fulton's *Clermont,* which made its appearance in 1807.

Our industrialized world owes more to James Watt than to any other man. For it was his steam engine that gave the Industrial Revolution its first power. Other men have since improved it, but it was Watt's invention that first gave man an efficient and practical means of harnessing steam.

ELI WHITNEY

(1765–1825)

The Cotton Gin Revolutionizes an Industry

I N 1793 the inventive genius of a Yankee school teacher made cotton "king" of the southern United States. Eli Whitney constructed the first practical cotton gin on a plantation at Mulberry Grove, Georgia, on June 1, 1793.

Before this eventful day seeds had to be picked from the cotton fibers by hand or with crude, manually operated machines, both laborious operations that produced little "clean" cotton for use in the mills. Whitney's machine, which could be operated by horsepower or waterpower, could easily clean 100 pounds of cotton or more a day, an amount equal to the output of 50 men using the old methods.

Cotton was a minor crop in the South prior to Whitney's invention. Southern agriculture at that time was based primarily on the production of rice, tobacco, corn, and turpentine. In 1793, for instance, barely 200,000 pounds of cotton were produced. Today the United States is the world's largest cotton-growing country. And this multi-billion dollar industry evolved directly from the invention of a Yankee mechanic.

Eli Whitney was born on December 8, 1765 in Westborough, Massachusetts, about 40 miles from Boston. On the family farm in Worcester County, Eli's father had a combination workshop and forge. Whitney's mechanical talents soon became evident, and during the Revolutionary War, while still a youth, he started a business on the farm making hand-forged nails.

He was most adept with tools, and could contrive almost any mechanical gadget that was needed around the house.

In order to obtain a formal education he taught school in the one-room school house in the area during the winter months and attended nearby Leicester Academy in the summer. In 1789 his father sent him to Yale in New Haven, and he completed his education with the idea of becoming a teacher. A position was found for him as private tutor to a family in South Carolina, but the job fell through. Meanwhile he had made friends with Mrs. Nathaniel Greene, the widow of the Revolutionary War general, and the manager of her plantation, Phineas Miller. They invited him to live on the plantation at Mulberry Grove, Georgia, with the idea in mind that he would study law. His invention of the cotton gin changed this plan.

England at this time dominated the cotton textile industry. Hargreaves, Crompton, and Arkwright had perfected machines for manufacturing cotton cloth in previously unparalleled amounts, but their inventions were closely guarded secrets. It was not until 1789 that the American cotton industry was born, a short four years before Whitney invented his gin. Clean cotton was the problem facing all the mills; the old methods of separating the seeds from the fibers were insufficient to produce enough cotton to satisfy the appetites of these new machines.

Early in 1793, in just ten days time, Eli Whitney solved this problem.

It is not known who first suggested the idea of building a more practical cotton gin to Whitney, but the subject was a common topic of conversation in most Southern households of the time. Everyone grew cotton to make clothes for their families and slaves, but little was grown for export because of the great difficulty in ginning. At any rate, Whitney attacked the problem late in May of 1793, and by the first of June had actually constructed the first working model of his gin. In a letter to his father he said: "I made one before I came away which required the labor of one man and with which one man can clean ten times as much cotton as he can in any other way. This machine will be turned by water or with a horse and will do more than 50 men can with the old machines."

The older ginning machines referred to were roller gins which were powered by a single hand crank and somewhat resembled a clothes wringer. Whitney's cotton gin had a revolving cylinder to which a stationary wire cage was attached. The cylinder contained hundreds of short hooks which revolved close to the cage and literally tore the fiber that was in the cage from the seeds. A brush arrangement swept the fiber from the hooks while the seeds, stopped by the wire, dropped into a hopper. The cylinder could be geared for either horsepower or waterpower.

Whitney entered into partnership with Miller and returned to New Haven to construct the gins. He was awarded a patent, which was signed by President George Washington, on March 14, 1794. During the next four years Whitney built many gins in his shop in New

Haven, but the firm of Miller and Whitney was never a great success, mainly because others infringed on his patent rights and built copies of his invention.

But the story of Eli Whitney's inventive genius does not end with the failure of his business. His next contribution to the Industrial Revolution in the United States was almost as great as his cotton gin. He laid the foundation for the principle of manufacturing parts which were standard and readily interchangeable from one finished product to the next.

In 1798, after the cotton gin business had failed, Whitney was looking for some other manufacturing business to enter when the government appropriated a large sum of money for the manufacture of muskets in this country.

Prior to this time the United States Army had been almost entirely dependent on arms imported from abroad. Whitney was given a contract for 10,000 stand of musket, an unheard of figure for that time. He built his factory at Mill Rock near New Haven, and employing his new method of manufacturing interchangeable parts for the muskets, established a business that continued to supply arms to the United States Army long after his death in 1825. The firm was later purchased by the Winchester Arms Company.

Whitney's work left its mark on both agriculture and industry. His cotton gin brought about the rapid expansion of the southern United States while his method of standardization of machined parts gave to the North the foundation by which it became a giant.

ROBERT FULTON

(1765–1815)

Steam Replaces Sails

THE steamboat came of age in August of 1807 when "Fulton's Folly" began a successful round trip up the Hudson River from New York to Albany. The paddle-wheeled *Clermont* built by Robert Fulton made the 300-mile round trip in 62 hours — a remarkable speed for the day and age. And from that day on the sailing vessel, which had served man for more than 3,000 years, was on its way out.

Fulton was not the first man to build a steamboat, but because his was the first to operate successfully on a commercial basis, he is generally considered the inventor of this method of transportation. Like most other inventors, he readily borrowed from and improved upon the ideas and experiments of others before him. But where other men had failed to make the steamboat practical, Fulton succeeded.

Fulton was born November 14, 1765, on a farm in Little Britain Township, Pennsylvania. As a youth he showed aptitude as a painter, and at the age of 21 went to London to study art. He was a good artist, and many of his miniatures and portraits still exist today. But he lost interest in painting except as a hobby, and soon turned his talents to the field of invention. He became interested in the English canal system, and devised many improvements in canal construction and operation, and even wrote a treatise on canal navigation. It was during this period, 1793, that he first showed an interest in steamboats.

It is little known that Fulton's first venture in boat construction was the building of a submarine. From London he went to Paris where he was commissioned by the French government to construct a submarine to be used against the English. Using many of the ideas that David Bushnell had incorporated in his submarine, the *Turtle*, which was built in 1776 in New York and used to attack the English warship *Eagle*, Fulton designed, built, and operated a successful submarine.

His *Nautilus* was 21 feet long and six feet in diameter and was propelled by a hand-cranked screw. In July of 1801 Fulton, with a crew of three aboard, successfully tested his boat. The *Nautilus* could submerge to a depth of 25 feet and stay under water for a period of three hours, and travel at a speed of a little more than a mile an hour. This early submarine was a far cry from the present day nuclear-powered *Nautilus*, but it was a success. With his crude submarine Fulton even managed to torpedo (a word he coined) a large sloop anchored in the French harbor of Brest. The torpedo Fulton used was a kind of underwater floating mine set off by clockwork, but it accomplished the trick. Despite the success of his submarine, the French government lost interest in the project, and

Fulton turned his talents to the task of building a steamboat.

While living in Paris Fulton had become friendly with Robert Livingston, the United States minister to France. Livingston, one of the five men who had drafted the Declaration of Independence, was also interested in the steamboat. In 1798 he had persuaded the legislature of the state of New York to grant him exclusive rights to navigate steamboats in that state, providing he could build one to certain specifications. He succeeded in building a steamboat, but the vessel did not meet the specifications and he gave up the venture.

But Livingston's interest was aroused again when he met Fulton. In 1803 they agreed to build an experimental boat at their joint expense. Fulton went to work, and in August of that year his first steamboat ran successfully on the Seine River in Paris. This forerunner of the *Clermont* was 66 feet long, eight feet wide, and was propelled by two steam operated paddle wheels. After this success the two men decided that Fulton should return to New York and build a larger steamboat which would be commercially practical. Livingston also persuaded the New York legislature to extend to himself and Fulton the same exclusive rights to operate steamboats in New York state as they had done in 1798.

Fulton contracted to have the engines of the *Clermont* built in England by the firm of Boulton and Watt. But it was not until 1806 that they arrived in New York. Fulton then went to work on the hull of his boat, which was built in the shipyard of Charles Brown on the East

River. The *Clermont* was 130 feet long, sixteen-and-a-half feet wide, and four feet deep. The boiler of the engine, which was mounted on the deck, was twenty feet long, and the furnace was fired with pine wood. Besides her two paddle wheels, which were fifteen feet in diameter, the *Clermont* was equipped with two small masts and a bowsprit, making her look much like a conventional sailing sloop of the day. But the large deck cabin, towering smokestack, and churning paddle wheels proclaimed this to be an entirely different type of vessel.

On Monday, August 11, 1807, the *Clermont* began her historic run to Albany, and a new chapter was begun in the history of transportation. With clouds of black smoke billowing up from her smokestack, the *Clermont* sailed majes-tically up the Hudson to the astonishment of the thousands of persons who flocked to the riverbank to witness this great event.

In a few short years this sight was common-place, and steamboats were plying every river and lake in the country — and in most parts of the world. Shortly afterward the steamboat ventured to sea, first as a coastal vessel and then, in 1819, the steamship *Savannah* made the first transatlantic crossing. With this feat steam demonstrated its superiority over the sail, and soon the colorful sailing vessels were no more.

Fulton, however, did not live to see the tremendous results his invention had wrought. He died in 1815, but the contributions he made to mankind surely mark him as one of the *Giants of Invention*.

GEORGE STEPHENSON

(1781–1848)

The Railroad Comes of Age

WITH THE advent of the steam engine late in the 18th century, men began to seek ways to adapt this new source of power to transportation as well as industry. In 1807 Robert Fulton built the first successful steamboat, and seven years later George Stephenson constructed the first practical steam locomotive. These two inventions revolutionized the modes of travel and transportation of goods between distant places.

Stephenson has often been called the "father of the locomotive," but this is not the whole story. The locomotive he invented in 1814 was the first to run efficiently on rails and to be operated profitably on a commercial basis. It might be more fitting to call him the "father of the railroad". It was Stephenson who surveyed the roadbed, laid the track, and built the locomotives for the first railroad built expressly for the purpose of hauling freight and passengers.

George Stephenson was born June 9, 1781, in a humble cottage in Wylam, England. His father was a firemen on one of the steam engines used to pump water from a nearby mine, and George often accompanied his father to work and became familiar at an early age with the workings of steam engines. He also became familiar with the wooden railway on which horse-drawn carts were employed to haul coal from the mines.

Young George did not attend school as a boy. Instead, at the age of 14 he was employed as an assistant stoker on his father's pumping engine. His interest in machinery and natural talent for mathematics drove him, at the age of 18, to educate himself. By the time he was 21 he had taught himself to read and write and became proficient in mathematics. He then moved to the village of Killingsworth, where his mechanical ability won him the job of engine-wright for the mines located there. His skill became even more apparent as he improved the pumping equipment as well as the wooden railways used to haul the coal from the mine to a nearby port.

Stephenson had seen a crude locomotive used at another mine, which was ineffective because it kept smashing the wooden rails, and decided he could build a better one. With the financial assistance of the mine owner, he began to construct his first locomotive in 1813. By July 25, 1814, the *Blucher* made a successful run, pulling a load of 30 tons of coal uphill at a speed of four miles an hour. His success lay as much in the rails he designed as it did in the well-built locomotive. His edged rails, which kept the engine on the track, were the forerunners of the type used on railroads today.

After this success, Stephenson built several

more locomotives of the *Blucher* type, each an improvement over the last. During this period he also built an eight-mile railway for the nearby Hetton Colliery, gaining experience which was to aid him in the construction of the first railroad.

In 1821 a group of promoters in Darlington, a city in the north of England, proposed building a railroad beginning some nine miles west of that city, which would run through it to the river port of Stockton, a distance of 20 miles. Stephenson was commissioned to do the job. He surveyed the route with his son Robert, then supervised the construction of the roadbed and the laying of the iron rails. With several partners he opened a factory in Newcastle to build the locomotives needed for the Stockton and Darlington Railroad. He also built the first passenger coach ever used on a railroad.

On the 27th of September, 1825, the first railroad went into operation. The *Locomotion*, as the engine was called, thundered through the North England countryside, shooting up clouds of black smoke and streams of sparks as it pulled its 30 cars and 300 passengers along at speeds up to 15 miles an hour.

With this success, Stephenson's fame spread throughout England and the world. His locomotive factory flourished, and his help was sought to construct many of the railroads lines which began to spring up throughout England, including the Liverpool and Manchester Railroad. For this line, completed in 1830, he built what is considered his most famous locomotive, the *Rocket*.

Up to the time of his death in 1848, Stephenson and his son Robert continued to build railroads, locomotives, and rolling stock. His products were as sturdy as his character. And if he was not exactly the "father of the locomotive," he was indeed the first and finest railroad man the world ever knew.

SIR HUMPHRY DAVY

(1778–1829)

Davy Lights the Way

THE expansion of the coal industry which supplied fuel for the growing Industrial Revolution in England in the early 19th century was made possible by the simple invention of a miner's lamp. Explosions of "pit gas" caused by the miner's torches were resulting in many deaths, slowing the production of coal needed to fuel the engines of industry. In desperation the miners turned to Sir Humphry Davy, one of the most celebrated chemists in the world, and in three short months he produced the safety lamp so urgently needed.

That Davy should accomplish the trick in so short a time was no surprise to the English. By 1815 this talented and charming young chemist had already captivated his countrymen and the rest of the world with his scientific achievements.

Davy was born in Cornwall on December 17, 1778, the son of a wood carver. After a brief schooling he was apprenticed at the age of 15 to an apothecary. Here he became acquainted with chemistry, and completed his education by reading the works of the leading philosophers, scientists, and mathematicians of the day. His investigations into the subjects of heat and light brought the youth to the attention of one Dr. Beddoes, who operated a medical research institute, and Davy was offered the job of laboratory director.

It was here that Davy launched his career as a chemist. His discovery at the age of 20 that nitrous oxide (laughing gas) had anesthetic value brought his first taste of fame, although it was another 50 years before physicians made use of his discovery. This led to a position as laboratory director and assistant professor of chemistry at the Royal Institution in London.

Here Davy's genius flourished. His lectures on chemistry caught the fancy of London society, and the "boy wonder" was lionized. He was slovenly both in manner and dress, but his natural charm made him the most sought after man in London. His laboratory, as well as his living quarters, was in a constant state of confusion, but despite his careless habits he became one of the world's greatest chemists.

Davy's accomplishments were many. He was the first to demonstrate that water could be decomposed by passing an electric current through it, and founded the science of electro-chemistry. He decomposed the fixed alkalis to their metallic nature, naming them potassium and sodium, and discovered and named the element chlorine. While traveling in France, and using only a portable chemical kit, he discovered and named "iodine". He pioneered in industrial chemistry and agricultural chemistry, and in an entirely different field, invented the arc light in 1808.

Davy's fame today probably rests more upon his important discoveries in chemistry than upon his invention of the safety lamp, but in his day the invention was regarded as of such outstanding importance to Britain's industry that he received the title of baronet as a result of it.

Davy made no effort to patent his invention nor to make money from it. All he received was a present from the mine owners of a set of silver dinner service. He ordered that after his death this be melted and sold, the proceeds being used to establish the annual award of a medal for chemical discoveries. The medal is still being given.

The invention came three years after Davy had retired as profesor of chemistry at the Royal Institute in 1812. Upon his retirement, he married and set out upon a tour of Europe.

Even on his honeymoon, however, he found plenty of scientific interests to occupy his attention, and he even took along a scientific assistant, Michael Faraday, to help him write up his experiments. Among his discoveries during his tour was that the diamond is composed of carbon and will burn in pure oxygen. Even though England and France were at war, so great was his fame that he was received with honors in Paris.

With all his success, however, this brilliant scientist and inventor did not succeed in one pursuit that meant almost as much to him as his researches. Davy wanted to be a great poet; and he wrote poetry throughout his life. Even so the breadth of his talent was such that the poet Coleridge was prompted to say of him that had he "not been the first chemist, he would have been the first poet of his age."

MICHAEL FARADAY

(1791-1867)

His Dynamo Electrified the World

A T the beginning of the 19th century the nature of electricity was a baffling mystery to scientists. They devoted a great amount of their time probing the nature of electricity, in much the same way that physicists of today devote most of their time probing the nature of the atom.

That we can take electricity so much for granted today is due to the success of these early scientists in unraveling the mystery of electricity and in putting this force to use. Of all these men, none have had a greater effect upon modern life than Michael Faraday, the discoverer of the dynamo.

Born in a small town near London, the son of a poor blacksmith, Faraday became one of the most respected scientists of his time — "the greatest experimenter of the 19th century." Without Faraday's discoveries in the relation of electricity and magnetism, the only sources of power would still be the steam engine, windmills, draft animals, and human muscle.

Our modern knowledge of electricity actually began in 1870 when an Italian physician named Luigi Galvani noticed that the leg of a frog he was dissecting twitched convulsively whenever he touched an exposed nerve with his scapel. Surprised and puzzled by this unexpected sign of life, Galvani sought for the cause of the twitching. He discovered that the leg muscle would contract whenever he touched the nerve with one kind of metal while the leg muscles were being touched by another kind of metal.

Searching for an explanation, Galvani decided that the nerves of the dead frog must contain some kind of a "vital fluid" that controlled muscular movement. Whenever the nerves and muscles happened to come into contact with two different kinds of metal, the "vital fluid" was released and the muscles would contract.

Galvani described his experiments in a paper published in 1791. Intrigued by Galvani's discovery, another Italian, a professor of physics at the University of Pavia whose name was Alessandro Volta, repeated Galvani's experiments. Volta came to the conclusion that a "vital fluid" had nothing to do with the twitching muscle. The muscle had moved because the nerve had been excited by an electric shock. The electricity had come from the touching of the two dissimilar metals.

To prove his statement, Volta built a simple device which was the ancestor of the battery. He stacked a pile of thin copper and zinc discs upon each other, alternating a copper disc with a zinc disc. Between each pair of copper and zinc discs he placed a piece of cloth soaked with salt water. When he connected a copper wire to each end of his stack and touched the wires together, a current of electricity flowed through the wire.

When Volta announced that he had found a way of producing a current of electricity, intense excitement gripped scientists throughout Europe. The existence of static electricity had been known to scientists for a long time. They knew that static electricity could be stored in Leyden jars and discharged as sparks. But that electricity could be "stored" in chemicals and made to flow continuously through wires was a momentous discovery. Scientists everywhere built "voltaic piles" — as Volta's stack of discs came to be called — to experiment with this new electricity and discover its properties.

One of these scientists was a Danish professor of physics named Hans Christian Oersted. One day in 1820 Oersted was giving a demonstration on the properties of electricity to a group of students. He was using as his source of electricity a voltaic pile. When he happened to place a magnetic compass close to the wire coming from the voltaic pile, he was surprised to see the compass needle swing until it was pointing towards the wire. When Oersted reversed the connections to the voltaic pile, the needle swung about in the opposite direction. Oersted had discovered by accident that a current flowing through a wire had magnetic properties.

Michael Faraday was deeply interested in Oersted's new discoveries. He was then 29 years old and had been working in the laboratory of the Royal Institution in London since he was 20. Faraday was the protege of Sir Humphry Davy, the famous English chemist. As a young man Faraday had built a small voltaic pile, using seven copper halfpennies, seven discs of sheet zinc, and six pieces of paper moistened with salt water. With this homemade equipment, he had decomposed sulfate of magnesia. Impressed with Faraday's honest personality and his experiments, Davy had taken the young man into his laboratory as his assistant. Years later, When Davy was asked what his most important discovery had been, he replied, "Michael Faraday."

In his laboratory at the Royal Institution, Faraday felt certain that if an electric current could influence a magnet, then a magnet should be able to influence an electric current. Perhaps it might even be possible to convert magnetism into electricity? Faraday attempted several experiments to see if this could be done but none of his experiments were successful.

During the next 11 years, Faraday made many attempts to convert magnetism into electricity but all his efforts came to nothing. Instead, he took up other interests of his, electroplating and electrolysis — the decomposition of chemicals when an electric current is passed through them.

In fact, the words *electrolysis, electrolyte, electrode, anode* and *cathode* were all used first by Faraday. But during this time he never gave up his belief that magnetism could be converted into electricity. In fact, he is supposed to have always carried a small magnet and a coil of wire in his pocket to remind him of his problem.

Faraday finally decided to attempt another series of experiments. He made a ring out of a soft iron rod. Around one half of the ring he wound a coil of wire and connected the ends of the coil to a galvanometer. If any current flowed through the coil, the needle of the galvanometer would swing to one side. Faraday then wound another coil of wire around the other half of the iron ring. The coils did not touch. When he connected the ends of the second coil to a battery, nothing seemed to happen. Disappointed, Faraday disconnected the battery. But as he did so, he noticed that the needle on a galvanometer flicked slightly. Curious, he connected the coil to the battery again. Again the galvanometer needle flicked slightly.

Excited now, Faraday tried another experiment. He wound a coil of wire around a paper tube and connected the ends of the coil to his galvanometer. When he inserted a steel magnet into the tube, the needle flicked. When he withdrew the magnet, the needle flicked again. Faraday tried many other experiments, always with the same result. As long as either the wire coil or the magnet was in motion, electricity was induced in the wire coil. Faraday had finally succeeded.

Faraday continued his experiments. He realized that if an electric current could be induced in a wire coil only when there was movement between the magnet and the coil, then the way to generate electricity continuously was to have a continuous movement between the two.

Faraday built a simple piece of equipment to test this idea. He mounted a disc of copper on a shaft so that the disc could be revolved by means of a handle. He connected his galvanometer to the disc with two wires, one wire touching the shaft and the other wire touching the edge of the disc. He then placed the copper disc between the poles of a horseshoe magnet and turned the handle. The needle of the galvanometer swung to one side and remained there as long as Faraday continued to turn the handle. Faraday had built the first dynamo.

Faraday announced his discoveries in lectures before the Royal Institution during the winter of 1831-2. After he had demonstrated his dynamo, someone in the audience asked him of what use was it. Faraday replied, "Of what use is a baby?"

Faraday's invention has indeed proved useful. His simple hand-operated machine is the forerunner of the giant turbogenerators that supply almost all the electrical energy consumed today.

When he found his mental powers failing in old age, Faraday retired from his laboratory because he could no longer maintain the high standards he had set for himself. He had given all his discoveries freely to the world, refusing to capitalize on his work. It was 54 years since he had first entered the laboratory of the Royal Institution — Davy's greatest discovery.

LOUIS DAGUERRE

(1789–1851)

Photography Joins the World of Art and Science

A French painter is responsible for giving photography to the world. In 1837 Louis Daguerre developed a process for obtaining permanent pictures which were called daguerreotypes. The world greeted the announcement of this new invention with astonishment, skepticism, and even scorn, but soon afterward there were as many "daguerreotype bugs" as there are "camera bugs" today.

Daguerre was not, however, the first man to make a photograph. He was joined by another Frenchman, Nicéphore Niepce, a pioneer in the field since 1814 with whom Daguerre formed a partnership. Other early pioneers in this field included a trio of Englishmen, Sir Humphry Davy, Thomas Wedgewood, and Fox Talbot.

Daguerre was born in Cormeilles, a small town ten miles from Paris. He had little formal education, but early showed a talent for drawing. At the age of thirteen his parents apprenticed him to an architect, and for three years the young Daguerre was trained as a draftsman. But the boy was determined to become an artist, and prevailed upon his parents to let him go to Paris to study.

After years of study Daguerre made a success not as a painter, but as a stage designer. In Paris he opened a "Diorama", a new type of theater entertainment which consisted of an exhibition of transparent paintings under changing lighting effects. Complete with sound effects, the "Diorama" was billed as the moving picture theater of its day.

It was during this period, around 1826, that Daguerre became obsessed with the idea of fixing permanently the image of the camera. The cameras of his day were crude wooden boxes with a single lens. Images could then be made on paper or plates coated with silver chloride. But these early pictures could not be made permanent and the image would blacken shortly after the picture was taken.

For two years Daguerre closeted himself in a laboratory he had built in the back of his Diorama, studying chemistry and experimenting with different types of plates. He was so absorbed in this work that he neglected almost everything else, although his Diorama continued to operate successfully, providing him with a most comfortable living. At one point his wife became so upset with his preoccupation that she approached a well-known scientist of the day and asked his advice. "My husband is possessed with the idea that he can fix the image of the camera and spends all his time trying to accomplish this idea. Can this be done, or do you think him mad?" The scientist replied: "Madam, with the knowledge we possess today it cannot be done. But it is possible, and I would not say that the man who seeks to accomplish this is mad."

Daguerre certainly was not mad. He contin-

ued his experiments, and in 1829 he formed a partnership with Niepce, who was also seeking to capture the illusive image of the camera, and who had already succeeded in making a permanent photograph. Niepce, however, was unable to devise a process that was practicable. The two men continued their experiments for several years, but Niepce died in 1832 and Daguerre was forced to carry on alone. Painstakingly, step by step, he experimented with various chemicals to coat his plates. Finally he found that iodide of silver worked best as a coating, but was still unable to fix the image permanently. In May of 1837, however, he found the answer.

Daguerre used plates treated with iodide of silver. After a relatively short exposure time, he exposed the plates to vapor of mercury. He then fixed them in a solution of common salt and hot water. Later he substituted hyposulphite of soda for this solution, which worked even better. After eleven long years of frustration, Daguerre had managed to capture the image of the camera permanently, and the art of photography was born. He called his invention a daguerreotype, and graciously shared the profits of his invention with the heirs of his former partner.

Honors were heaped upon the inventor, and his invention was shown throughout the world. The French government made him a member of the Legion of Honor and bestowed upon him a pension of 6,000 francs a year for life. Daguerre revealed to the entire world what up to then had been a secret process, and since that time all mankind have benefited from the labors of this talented French painter.

There have been many improvements since the first daguerreotypes appeared in 1837. The process of developing pictures as we do today — from negatives — was invented in 1884 by George Eastman. In that year Eastman developed the roll film system, and a few years later gave the world the "Kodak" type camera which is in such wide use today. Motion pictures and colored photography soon followed. Improved cameras and film now permit the photographer, whether professional or amateur, to capture any image under almost any condition he might desire, and industry and science have adapted this refined form of "daguerreotypes" to their use.

It would be difficult to say that any one man alone had given the world one of its arts, but the point could be argued most successfully in the case of Louis Daguerre.

SAMUEL FINLEY BREESE MORSE

(1791–1872)

Man Communicates by Electricity

As it was in the case of many of the other great inventors, the "father of the telegraph" was an artist before he became an inventor. But despite the recognition he won for his portraits and paintings, it was not until 1836 that the invention of the telegraph made instant communication possible and made the name of Samuel Finley Breese Morse famous the world over.

Morse was born on April 27, 1791, in Charleston, Massachusetts, not far from the famed Breed's Hill of Revolutionary War days. His father was a clergyman, and managed to afford young Morse with a very liberal education for the times. At an early age he demonstrated his talents as a painter, and continued the study of art when he attended Yale University. But while at Yale he was equally interested in science and it was as a student that Samuel Morse first became interested in electricity. As a matter of fact, he first conceived the idea of a telegraph at Yale at the age of 19, but it was years later before the idea became an actuality.

However, the study of art was still his first love, and in 1811, after leaving Yale, he went to London to continue his studies. But even there, in his letters home to his father, the idea of the telegraph was in his thoughts, and he voiced the wish to his father that they could communicate more quickly over the 3,000 miles of ocean that

separated them. He returned to the United States in 1815, with some fame as a painter, but a poor man. He managed to eke out a living the next few years with his painting, by lecturing and writing, and opened the National Academy of Design in New York. During these years he was also becoming more and more obsessed with the idea of "making electricity write."

In 1827 Harrison Gray Dyer experimented with a crude telegraph system on Long Island in New York, but gave up the venture. Others at the same time were experimenting with electricity and the problem of telegraphy. The main obstacle at the time was the need for an effective battery to supply sufficient current to the line and for a relay to renew the power over long distances. Morse and the others knew that by breaking the circuit a spark was formed, but how to make this spark "talk" had them all baffled.

In 1829 Morse returned to Europe to paint. On his return to the United States aboard the sailing ship *Sully* he devised his first crude alphabet for making the spark "talk" by using dots and dashes to denote letters and numbers. Shortly after his arrival in New York he was made a professor of Literature at New York University, and at this time began experimenting in earnest to solve the problem of the telegraph. He improved the Morse code and his instruments. By that time

[51]

the Daniel battery had been invented to give a reliable source of power. In 1835 Morse invented the relay to solve still another of the problems, and in 1836 and again in 1837 he built instruments, which though still crude, operated successfully.

He continued experimenting, and improving to his system; in 1844 Morse induced the United States government to appropriate sufficient funds to permit a demonstration of the telegraph system on a grand scale. A line was built from Baltimore to Washington and the tests were made before the public and members of Congress. The line operated successfully, and telegraphy became man's first system of communication operated by electricity.

Morse offered his invention to the government for $100,000, but was refused. He then sold the rights to build telegraph lines to private investors, a company in Rochester, New York being the first to construct a privately owned telegraph system in the world. It took time for this new communication system to catch on, but soon lines connected the major cities of the country. The giant Western Union system was born. Morse's system was used to connect America with Europe when Cyrus W. Field laid the first transatlantic cable. Later in the century

such men as Thomas A. Edison made improvements on Morse's instruments. Edison invented the quadruplex telegraph which permitted the simultaneous transmission of four messages over one wire (two in each direction), greatly improving Morse's original instruments.

But it was Samuel Morse who fathered the telegraph, and it is to him the world owes its first system of almost instantaneous communication. Wireless telegraphy invented by Guglielmo Marconi years later owed a great debt to Morse's original invention, and it might even be said to have had a hand in the development of radio and television.

Although newer, and in some cases better,

systems of communication have been invented since 1836, Samuel Morse's telegraph is still one of man's major methods of communication.

Morse was honored more abroad than in his own country for his invention. European sovereigns showered honors on him. He was decorated by the sultan of Turkey, the king of Prussia, the king of Wurtemberg, and the emperor of Austria. The French made him a chevalier of the Legion of Honor; the king of Denmark and the queen of Spain also honored him with their highest awards. What was more important to Morse at the time was an award of 200,000 francs pooled by the major nations of Europe, for he had constant expenses in protecting his telegraph from patent infringement.

Morse continued to press his interest in science and invention. He became the first photographer in America, using the process invented in France by Daguerre.

ELIAS HOWE

(1819–1867)

Sewing Becomes Mechanized

A CONVERSATION overheard and the desire to ease his wife's burden of sewing by hand led Elias Howe to the invention of the sewing machine. But Howe had to suffer hardship and poverty before he was recognized as the inventor of the sewing machine and was able to realize the fruits of his invention.

Elias Howe was born in Spencer, Massachusetts, in 1819. His father was a farmer who also had a grist mill, a saw mill, and a machine for making shingles. Elias was born lame and was unable to do much work on the farm, but he showed an early interest in the machinery that operated his father's mills. This interest in mechanics led his father, when Elias was but 16, to apprentice the youth to a cotton factory in Lowell, Massachusetts, where he learned to repair the looms and other machinery used in the cotton mill.

After two years, however, the mill shut down, and Elias drifted to Boston. There he found employment in the shop of Ari Davis, who made and repaired instruments of all kinds. It was in this shop, in 1839, that Howe overheard the conversation which was partly responsible for his inventing the sewing machine. A customer in the shop was talking to Davis about a knitting machine he was trying to make. "Why bother about a knitting machine," Davis said. "Why not make a sewing machine?"

"It can't be done," the customer answered, "it's impossible to get a needle to stitch downward through the cloth and then back up again."

"Nonsense," Davis snorted. "I could do it myself if I had time. Some sort of contraption using two needles — one above and one beneath the cloth."

Due to a lack of time Davis did not invent the sewing machine. But he had the right idea. Howe was impressed by the idea, but gave it little thought until after he was married. His wife was in poor health and the task of making clothes for Elias and their three children was almost too much for her. It was while watching her at her needlework one night that Howe recalled the conversation he had overheard in Davis' shop. A sewing machine! I'll make one, he thought, and make life a little more comfortable for her.

He began his experiments in 1843, quitting his job to devote his full time to inventing a sewing machine. Ironically, his poor wife's work was doubled as she had to take in sewing to support the family. Howe had no knowledge of the sewing machines which had been invented before he entered the field. There had been several crude machines invented, including that of Thomas Saint of England in 1790 and one built by Barthélemy Thimmonier of France in 1830. An American, Walter Hunt, had invented a machine in 1834, but little had come of it.

Howe clung to the idea of using two needles, and independently invented an improved machine whose principle is still used today. The greatest problem he had to solve was what kind of needles to use and how to combine them to make a continuous stitch. He solved the problem by using a needle with the eye at the point above the cloth. The needle below the cloth served as a shuttle, and the two threads were combined to form a lockstitch. The operation of the bottom needle was similar to that of a shuttle and loom.

The sewing machine was patented in 1846,

but it was not until 1854 that Howe reaped any benefits from his invention. During that period many persons put machines on the market which infringed on Howe's patent. Some improved on the original, particularly the machine manufactured by Isaac Singer. Singer added a foot-operated treadle instead of the hand wheel of Howe's machine, which left both of the operator's hands free while sewing.

Howe, who had taken out a patent in England as well as in the United States went to England in 1847 where he sold all his English rights in the invention to a corset manufacturer for $1250. When he returned to the United States he was

broke and went back to work as a mechanic.

He had drawn up his American patent with great skill and he set about to assert his rights against the several companies that were now making sewing machines. By 1855 there were three major companies in the field and each was claiming that the others were infringing their patents. Howe was able, however, to make a very strong case that all were infringing upon his rights.

The matter was settled very much to his advantage when all the companies agreed to drop their suits and to pay a royalty to Howe for every machine sold. These royalties at times amounted to as much as $4,000 a day.

Thus the crippled farm boy became a wealthy man, and his invention, made to ease the burden of his wife's work, made sewing an easy task for millions of women. The great revolution it wrought, however, was in the garment industry, where today hundreds of specialized kinds of sewing machines perform the many different jobs necessary to turn out clothing.

SIR HENRY BESSEMER

(1813–1898)

The Age of Steel

THE cannon roared and the shot flew true. Again the gun was loaded with one of the new, elongated shells and again it scored a bull's-eye on the target located on the artillery range on the outskirts of Paris. "The shots rotate properly," the French artillery officer said to the young English inventor, "but if you cannot find a stronger metal to build guns with, such heavy projectiles as you have invented will be of little use."

Sir Henry Bessemer listened to the French officer's words and he determined to find a way to produce a metal from which such guns as the officer had described could be cast. But instead of developing a metal for making stronger cannons, he invented a process for making cheap steel that put new life into the Industrial Revolution then under way in England and Europe. By doing so he ushered in the Age of Steel.

Until Bessemer perfected his method in 1856, making steel was a long and costly process. By the old method of using a "puddling furnace" to convert pig iron into steel the cost per ton was about $250. Bessemer's process reduced the cost to $50 a ton.

In his efforts to produce a better metal for guns, Bessemer almost exhausted the fortune he had amassed from other inventions, particularly a process for making bronze dust to be used in paint. For this new venture he first built an orthodox puddling furnace with which to ex-

periment. In this furnace pig iron was stirred or "puddled" so that the flame and air could reach all parts of the molten iron and eventually turn the mass into steel. One day, quite by accident, the inventor discovered that if air was forced into the molten pig iron under great heat the iron would turn to steel in a matter of minutes. He decided that if this happened when great heat was applied to the molten pig iron, it might also happen without this heat, and would further reduce the cost of making the steel. He designed and built what he called a "converter" for this experiment. The converter was pear-shaped and had pipes built into the bottom, through which air could be forced. When all was ready he poured molten pig iron into the converter and then pumped air into the liquid metal. As in the previous experiment, the result was steel in a matter of minutes instead of hours — and without having to use extra fuel to create heat under the converter. The Bessemer process for making steel was born, and instead of being used primarily to make better cannons this new process was used to build more and better ships, locomotives, rails, bridges, buildings, tools, and the innumerable other things steel is used for. As happens often when man has a great need for a new tool or a new way of doing something, a similar process for making cheap steel was being developed in the United States about the same time as Bessemer perfected his method. William

[59]

Kelly developed the process in America and was given the patent rights in the United States, but Sir Henry Bessemer is generally credited with the steel-making method that bears his name.

At first Bessemer's method was not accepted by the steel makers of England, mainly because the pig iron used was inferior. But after four more years of experimenting, Bessemer found a solution to this problem and he was hailed as a genius. His fortune was made, and he was knighted by the king of England. Other men have since developed other and perhaps better ways of making steel, but it was Sir Henry Bessemer who gave the world the Age of Steel.

NIKOLAUS OTTO

(1832-1891)

He Made Power Mobile

From grocery clerk to traveling salesman to inventor — that was the unlikely route traveled by Nikolaus August Otto, inventor of the four-cycle internal combustion engine.

Born in the tiny country town of Holzhausen auf der Heide, on the Rhine, Germany, in 1832, Otto seemed hardly to have the background for world-changing invention. He was bright enough, scoring the highest grades as far as he went in high school. But he didn't go very far.

His father, Philip Wilhelm Otto, was an innkeeper who held the office of postmaster in their little community. He died soon after Nikolaus was born, leaving his widow to get on as best she could. Insecure, she felt that Nikolaus would make out better in business than in taking the long road to education and learning. So the boy was taken from his high school desk and placed behind a grocery counter.

The small town grocery proved too tight a container for young Otto's lively spirit and he moved on to a short period of clerical work in Frankfort. Again he was bound too tightly by his surroundings. His brother in Cologne got him a job as a traveling salesman. In this position, at least, he was able to move about the countryside, chatting with shopkeepers in the villages and towns. Then he would return to the more industrial city of Cologne.

At a gay country carnival he met a girl named Anna Gossi. They went together and fell in love

— but for the present Otto was far too poor to consider marriage. What he was considering, as a matter of fact, was mechanics. His brain was filled with ideas of power and motion. Engines had somehow become his preoccupation as he talked of the prices of condiments and cheese.

What was the state of engine power in the world at that time? The steam engine had been in existence for more than a hundred years. The wheels of the major factories of the world were driven by steam, as were locomotives on land and great ships at sea.

But there existed no source of mechanical power for craftsmen and smaller manufacturers; no way to drive smaller vehicles except through the use of animals.

A Frenchman named Lenoir had, in 1860, produced a workable gas engine. It operated somewhat like the steam engine which it resembled in design, and was driven by explosions of a mixture of gas and air.

This engine caused much excitement in the scientific and industrial world, but it proved to be no more than an introduction to future possibilities. It was uneconomic and inefficient — a great idea, but not of much use practically.

Otto had been thinking of it as he traveled the dusty country roads. He knew the explosive quality of the vapors of petroleum spirits and other liquid hydrocarbons. Why couldn't these be used to power an explosive-type engine? Wouldn't that be more efficient than dependence upon gas lines — lines which existed only in certain limited areas in any case?

He sketched a design and took it to Michael Zons, a man who operated a machine shop in Cologne. From this design Zons constructed a primitive "carburetor." Fumes of heated alcohol were to be piped to a cylinder to drive a piston by explosive force. Neither man knew that the idea had already been patented. But Otto was determined, in spite of his disappointment, to invent an engine which would, as he said, "propel vehicles serviceably and easily along country roads, as well as prove useful for the purposes of small industry."

Otto and Zons went on to construct a small engine along the lines of Otto's plan. In experimenting with the engine Otto conceived the idea of allowing a full stroke of the piston to fill the cylinder with the explosive mixture and utilize the next full stroke for compression, instead of half-strokes as had been done in Lenoir's model. The next stroke could then be used to produce the power, and the last stroke could exhaust the combustion products. In other words, he had conceived a four-cycle engine — a gigantic step forward.

It was still just an idea, but as he declared, he "cast all caution to the winds, and instead of a one-cylinder engine, I went right ahead and built one with four cylinders."

This was something that had never been thought of before. At the beginning of the year 1862 the project was realized. The only four-cycle engine ever to be seen in the world popped and blasted — and turned over for the first time.

Otto's exuberant enthusiasm matched the bucking of his banging engine. He spent every moment he could in Zons' machine shop. But progress was slow and he was forced to leave his salesman's job in order to devote enough time to his sputtering brain-child.

The engine needed his time. Violent knocking was knocking out its bearings. A thinner mixture produced less violent explosions, but only at the expense of constant misfiring.

While he contended with his misfirings, Anna, his girl, had to contend with her misgivings: Would he ever be successful? Would they ever get married? Would he ever find time to leave his fiendish engine and spend a little time with her?

Otto pounded and blundered on. He went over to London to see what they were doing there. Nothing new. No useful information. And so he came back to Cologne to continue his isolated journey on the road to a practical four-cycle engine.

Otto worked while Anna waited. He developed a new approach to driving his pistons with a weaker explosion. It was based on the atmospheric pressure principle used by James Watt in his first steam engines of a century before. After much experimental work the engine was made to operate.

But again he was granted no patent. The atmospheric principle was well known, he was told by the Ministry of Commerce in Berlin. He was granted patents by countries other than his own — England, France, Belgium — but it was difficult to make money from foreign patents. In Germany, where he might have seen some income from his work, his design was unprotected.

Consequently, he was obliged to work in secret. Still, the powerful pressure of poverty forced him to take the risk of offering his machine for sale to progressive craftsmen who understood the advantages this new source of power could give them.

Finally he received backing from an engineer named Eugen Langen. Langen opened a factory in Otto's name for the manufacture of the new engines.

Disappointment again. Many purchasers of the machines simply didn't have the skill it then took to keep them operating.

Otto and Langen worked on, firing their explosions into the teeth of failure. They developed a new gas engine model which they exhibited at the Paris World's Fair in 1867. The prize committee turned away from the noisy contraption with disgust. Again rejection and failure loomed.

However, the Prussian member of the prize jury was Professor Franz Reuleaux, an old friend of Langen. He insisted on a fair trial. For several days the committee picked the engine apart, analyzing its performance from every point of view.

Then, at a ceremony attended by Napoleon III, the gold medal was awarded to Otto and Langen. Their machine was a great success. It was greeted with enthusiasm by the press and the public.

Otto married his Anna, and from then on he and Langen produced model after model. There were ups and downs in business as well as in the experimental laboratory, but the two inventors kept going on.

Finally Otto perfected a four-cycle internal combustion engine that used liquid fuel and proudly bore his name. Other successful inventions followed, and Otto finally received the full measure of recognition he deserved.

The great partnership of Otto and Langen had borne abundant fruit. When Otto died in 1891, the two men had been working together for more than twenty-six years.

Theirs was a collaboration which left an indelible mark upon the world. All over the earth today the wheels of transportation, agriculture and industry turn upon the principles invented by Nikolaus Otto and Eugen Langen.

GEORGE WESTINGHOUSE

(1864–1914)

Safety Rides the Rails

THE idea for the invention of the air brake for railroad cars came from a magazine article concerning the construction of a railroad tunnel. George Westinghouse read the story and in a flash he had the solution to the problem of building better brakes for railroad cars. The tunnel was being dug with jack hammers driven by compressed air. Why not use compressed air to operate his brake?

Up to this time the brakes to control the thousands of cars used in the mushrooming railroad system in America were operated either mechanically or with steam. Neither method was very efficient or safe, and accidents were numerous. Westinghouse's air brake gave the railroads a safe and efficient means for controlling the speed of trains, permitting quick stops in emergencies. The invention was patented in 1869, and within five years almost every railroad car and locomotive in the United States was equipped with brakes built by the Westinghouse Air Brake Company.

George Westinghouse was one of the most prolific inventors of all time. In a period covering 48 years he took out more than 400 patents on devices ranging from his air brake to steam engines, electrical equipment, turbines, gas engines, and others. A tireless worker, his inventive genius in the period of 1880 — 1890 alone produced 134 patents.

He came by his inventive talent naturally. His father was also an inventor. George Westinghouse, Senior, operated a factory in Schenectady, New York, where he manufactured agricultural machinery. And although not as prolific an inventor as his son, he patented seven machines that he built in his shops. It was under his father's guidance that young George received his early training in mechanics and the use of tools. He was a poor student, more apt to play hookey than attend class. He was not lazy, but as a boy refused to do anything in which he was not interested. His father finally gave up his hope that George might become a scholar, and at the age of 14 put his son to work in the factory after school and on Saturdays at a wage of fifty cents a day to learn the trade. George was competely happy puttering about the factory and working in a laboratory he built for himself in the loft.

At 17 George enlisted in the Union Army, and at the end of the Civil War the youth returned to his father's factory and began his career as an inventor. In 1865, at the age of 19, he patented his first invention — a rotary steam engine. His interest in brakes for railroad cars came about through a disastrous train wreck in the area, and he took out some 20 patents on various types of brake apparatus before he invented his air brake in 1869.

The essential features of the air brake are an air pump operated by steam from the locomotive; a tank to hold compressed air with a valve for the engineer to operate; a line of pipe running from the tank under each car to each brake cylinder; and flexible hose connections between each car. The engineer operates the valve to admit air into the brake cylinders through the line, thus slowing or stopping the train. The system is essentially the same used on millions of railroad cars throughout the world today.

After the success of his air brake company, Westinghouse formed an electric company, inventing many of the products the firm manufactured. He, more than anyone else, is responsible for the development of the use of alternating current in America instead of direct current. The alternating current motor was developed in his plant by one of his engineers, Nikola Testa, and Westinghouse himself invented an incandescent lamp. He built everything, from the first generators used when Niagara Falls was harnessed to produce electricity, to trolley cars and steam turbines; he also pioneered in the field of the production and distribution of natural gas.

His empire grew, and the name Westinghouse is still one of the giants of the industrial world today, a living tribute to the boy who would rather play hookey than go to school — whose genius made our railroads safe and whose contributions to the electrical age are as near at hand as the closest light switch.

The Age of Modern Science

THOMAS ALVA EDISON

(1847-1931)

Electricity Becomes Man's Servant

THE inventive genius of a typical, self-made American individualist focused the attention of the world on America during the last quarter of the 19th century. Thomas Alva Edison left his imprint during this period as one of the most prolific inventors the world has ever known. He was acknowledged the leader of the "Electrical Age" for his practical contributions in communications, power, and light.

His inventions in the electrical field — the incandescent lamp, lighting and power systems, improvements to telegraphy — one of the most original inventions ever made, the phonograph, and one of the most influential, motion pictures, mark him as a genius whom the entire world honored during his lifetime. But with all the praise and glory heaped upon him, Edison remained a down-to-earth man, rich in human qualities — and not without his share of frailties.

Edison was born in Milan, Ohio on February 11, 1847, the son of Samuel and Nancy Elliot Edison. Sam Edison, who was a lumber and grain dealer, moved his family to Fort Gratiot on the outskirts of Port Huron, Michigan, when Tom was seven, and there the young Edison grew up. From this point on young Tom's life took on a Horatio Alger aspect. After only three months of formal education, Tom's mother, who had been a teacher before her marriage, took charge of her son's education. Nancy Edison sensed her son's real interest, and when he was

nine gave him his first elementary book on science. From that point on Edison read every scientific and technical book he could lay his hands on, and performed crude experiments in a laboratory he built in a corner of the cellar of their home. Here, too, he built his first working model of a telegraph, and strung a half-mile line of stovepipe wire to the house of a friend — they would sit up for hours sending and receiving messages.

When Edison was 12, the family fortunes began to ebb, and the need for money to buy the books and chemicals and equipment for his laboratory stimulated Edison to embark upon his first commercial enterprise. He and a friend raised vegetables and sold them in town, but, despite their success, Tom gave it up because as he recalled later ". . . hoeing corn in a hot sun is unattractive." His next venture to finance his experiments was more profitable and lasted longer. In 1859 the railroad came to Port Huron from Detroit, and Tom got the position of "candy butcher" on the run. Every morning at 7 a.m. he would begin the three hour ride to Detroit with a basket of candy, apples, sandwiches and a supply of newspapers to sell. For the next three years, until he was 15, Edison made this run morning and night, spending the intervening day investigating the machine shops and railroad yards of Detroit. During this period he had his "laboratory" in one corner of the baggage car, and continued his simple experiments and studies there.

But telegraphy had caught Tom's fancy, and his chance to become an operator, which in those days was as much of a boy's dream as becoming an astronaut is today, came through a lucky break. Tom rescued the young son of the station master at St. Clemens from the path of an on-coming freight train. The grateful station master, aware of Edison's desire, offered to teach him to be an operator. After mastering this new and exciting profession, Edison spent four years as a vagabond telegrapher, working throughout the Midwest and parts of the South.

In 1868 Edison gave up his job as an itinerant telegrapher and settled in Boston, finding work with Western Union as an operator. He grew bored with his job and, after borrowing money, set himself up as a free lance inventor and built a model of a multiplex telegraph apparatus that would send two messages over one wire. However, he could not get backing for it. It was during this period that the young inventor received his first patent for an invention — an electric vote recorder designed to accelerate the taking of votes in legislative bodies. But neither the Massachusetts Legislature nor Congress wanted any part of a machine that would upset the traditional prerogative of a minority to filibuster, and the disappointed inventor vowed that day never to invent anything that had no commercial demand.

Broke and heavily in debt, but not disheartened, Edison went to New York to try his luck. He soon found work as a mechanic with the Gold Indicator Company, which serviced brokerage offices in the city with the New York Stock Exchange quotations. Within a year his fortunes went from nothing to $40,000 as he sold his improved stock ticker to Western

Union. With this money the 23-year-old inventor set up his own shop and laboratory in Newark, New Jersey.

For the next five years Edison manufactured stock tickers and telegraphic equipment. He obtained numerous patents for new models of these machines, and finally invented an automatic telegraph and a quadruplex telegraph which would send four messages on one wire, two in each direction. This invention, one of the most important in the field of telegraphy, was the first to draw attention to the budding genius of the 27-year-old Edison.

ticker, promising to return by suppertime. It was midnight before an assistant happened to come upon Edison in the shop and apprised him of the time.

"Midnight," he said vaguely. "Is that so? I must get home then; I was married today."

In 1876, on a sudden whim, Edison decided to move his laboratory to Menlo Park, New Jersey, an isolated village some 25 miles from New York. He had decided to give up his manufacturing interests and to devote himself to the "invention business". This two story, barn-like building became the first industrial research

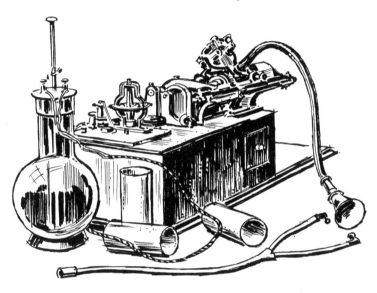

Edison was decidedly an egoist, but he knew how to win the affection and respect of the men he worked so hard in his shop. Once he locked himself and six of his men in the laboratory in Newark and told them that they could not leave the room until they had corrected a "bug" that had appeared in a new model of his stock printer. Sixty hours later they completed the job. But if he was a hard taskmaster, he was also very approachable and had a sense of humor that often led him to play practical jokes on his assistants. Although the shop was primarily kept busy with the manufacture of electrical apparatus, Edison would forget everything to experiment with a new idea. On the afternoon of his wedding to Mary Stilwell in 1871 he left his young bride to return to the laboratory in order to work out a technical problem on his stock

laboratory the world had ever known. Edison offered the services of his "invention factory" and his team of assistants for the purpose of making inventions to order. Western Union was one of the first to take advantage of the facilities at Menlo Park, and retained Edison to make improvements on Alexander Graham Bell's telephone. He responded by inventing a telephone transmitter that transformed Bell's crude telephone into a practical instrument of communication.

Edison's inventions up to this point had gained him recognition as a leading inventor of his day, but with his invention of the phonograph in 1877 he was regarded as a sheer wizard. While working on a model of a telegraph repeater, Edison was intrigued by the almost human sounds made by the high speed apparatus, and the idea occurred to him of making a "telephone repeater." Working toward that end, he completed a sketch of the machine in four months' time and ordered his assistant John Kruesi to make it. When Kruesi, a stolid but skilled German workman, returned with the model, he asked Edison what the machine was for.

"The machine must talk," Edison replied.

The simple machine was a 3½ inch cylinder mounted on a shaft with a hand crank to turn it. It had two diaphragms, each with a stylus, attached to opposite sides of the cylinder.

As Edison wrapped a sheet of tin foil around the cylinder, his assistants jokingly offered to bet him that the contraption would not work. Edison ignored them, and, turning the crank, shouted into one of the diaphragms:

Mary had a little lamb,
Its fleece was white as snow,
And everywhere that Mary went
The lamb was sure to go.

Then he adjusted the other diaphragm and stylus on the cylinder and again began to crank. Out of the machine came the voice of Edison reciting almost perfectly the Mother Goose rhyme. Kruesi turned pale and everyone present, including the inventor, stood dumbfounded. When news of the new "talking machine" got around, Edison's fame rose in leaps and bounds, but the "phonograph craze" resulting from this invention lasted only a year or so, and it was not until ten years later that the inventor turned his hand to improving his most original invention.

In 1878 the Wizard of Menlo Park became interested in the possibilities of electric lighting, and after studying the investigations and progress others had made in this field, decided he had a chance to invent a practical light before other inventors did. Working tirelessly, Edison and his assistants tested more than 1,600 different materials to find the one that would serve as the incandescent element for his sealed vacuum globes. Finally, on October 21, 1879, the breakthrough came as he experimented with a piece of carbonized thread as a filament which burned with a bright glow for 45 hours. He constructed a pilot light and power station at Menlo Park, and on New Year's eve of 1879 thousands gathered to see the new light.

Edison's fame throughout the world was almost unmatched as he became the acknowledged leader of the "Electrical Age." But the tireless inventor had little time to accept the plaudits of his admirers. He was busy getting

ready to light up New York City. The Edison Electric Light Company established headquarters in New York and began the gigantic task (for those times) of supplying light and power to lower Manhattan. The company had to design and build everything which the central system Edison envisioned would require — dynamos, switches, underground distribution mains, meters, and a whole family of lighting fixtures, sockets, and wiring. But the job was accomplished, and on September 4, 1882, the switch was pulled in the central station on Pearl Street. The world was truly given light.

Edison's inventions are too numerous to describe. During his lifetime he was awarded some 1,100 patents for his work. The list is wide and varied, including the motion picture camera, electric dynamos, electric locomotives, railway signal systems, the storage battery, an ore separator, and many more. He died on October 18, 1931, at the age of 84.

It was Thomas Alva Edison who applied the knowledge which science had been accumulating during the 19th century to make electricity a useful commodity that man could bend to his will, creating new industries, wealth, comfort and enjoyment — in fact, an entire new way of life.

ALEXANDER GRAHAM BELL

(1847–1922)

The Talking Wire

BOTH apparatuses were ready and the experiment was about to begin. Thomas Watson sat at a table laden with equipment and battery jars with his ear to the receiver and listened for the voice he hoped to hear over the wire connected to the instrument in the other room some 40 feet away. The first words were to be a line from Shakespeare: "To be or not to be, that is the question." All was quiet for a moment and then, instead of Shakespeare's immortal lines, Watson heard clearly and distinctly the words, "Mr. Watson, come here; I want you."

The voice Watson heard that March 10, 1876 was that of Alexander Graham Bell and his words heard over 40 feet of wire signalled that his invention of the telephone was a success. Watson rushed into the room in which Bell was waiting, shouting, "I could hear you! I could hear you!" Both men were so jubilant over their success that Bell almost forgot why he had summoned his assistant over the wire instead of quoting Shakespeare to him. It happened that while he was adjusting his equipment he had accidently spilled some of the acid from one of the battery jars on his clothing and in doing so had inadvertantly made the first emergency call over a telephone.

The 29-year-old inventor had conceived the idea of the telephone some two years before while working on an improvement to the telegraph, a device he called the multiple telegraph.

He had been able to find sufficient financial backing to complete this invention and patented it in April of 1875. While still working on the multiple telegraph Bell had become more and more obsessed with the idea of the telephone. But for this idea he could find practically no backing and had to go it alone except for the help of his faithful assistant Watson. Ironically, nothing came of Bell's multiple telegraph, whereas his telephone brought him a fortune, making almost instant communication to any part of the world readily available to the average citizen.

Alexander Graham Bell was born and educated in Edinburgh, Scotland. His father was a voice and speech teacher, and young Bell followed in his father's footsteps. In 1870 Professor Bell moved his family to Brantford, Canada, hoping that the climate of the New World would be more beneficial for young Alex, who was a frail youth. His parents feared he might die of consumption as had his two older brothers. The new life at Tupelo Heights on the outskirts of Brantford seemed to do the trick. Soon Alex left to teach and lecture on speech in Boston. He was particularly interested in aiding deaf and dumb children to learn to communicate and toyed with ideas of making a visible speech machine for this purpose.

This interest led him to the development of the multiple telegraph and then the telephone. By 1875 Bell had a good idea of what his telephone would be like, but was still unable to transmit discernible human speech over the wire. In March of 1875 he visited the leading American scientist of the times, Professor Henry of the Smithsonian Institute in Washington, D.C. The 80-year-old scientist was most impressed with Bell's theories of transmitting the human voice over wires. Bell asked Henry whether he should publish his findings at that time and let some one else perfect the invention, or whether he should keep at it himself. Henry strongly advised the young inventor to keep on with the work himself. When Bell said that he did not think he had sufficient electrical knowledge to continue, the old man replied dryly: "Get it!"

Bell did. He continued his experiments, trying to discover the kind of electric current necessary to transmit the human voice. On June 2, 1875 he found the key. He and Watson were working out some bugs in the multiple telegraph when accidentally the make-and-break points of a transmitter spring became welded together. When Watson plucked at them to separate the

two points they sent a distinct vocal sound over the wire. Bell, hearing the sound in the other room and seeing what Watson had done, immediately grasped the effect. It was simply that an electric current varying in intensity (an "undulatory current," Bell called it) could accomplish the transmission of human sounds while the intermittent current of telegraphy could not. It took Bell another year to perfect the telephone, but the job was done.

Bell demonstrated his invention publicly in 1876. Such famous persons as the Emperor of Brazil and Sir William Thomson, England's leading scientist, and Elisha Gray, who was one of Bell's leading competitors in the race to invent the telephone, listened and were awestruck by the magic of the talking wire. There was still much for Bell and his faithful Watson to do before the telephone would become as fixed an institution in the American home as the kitchen stove, but they had proved that man could send his voice over a wire.

OTTMAR MERGENTHALER

(1854–1899)

A Machine Revolutionizes Printing

THE ART OF printing owes as much, perhaps, to a German watchmaker as it does to the inventor of printing. For Ottmar Mergenthaler invented a typesetting machine that almost entirely did away with setting type by hand just as Johann Gutenberg, inventor of movable type and the printing press, made it no longer necessary to write books by hand.

Ottmar was born in Brelingheim in southern Germany on May 10, 1854. His parents wanted him to follow in the footsteps of "Papa" Mergenthaler, a lawyer, but Ottmar rebelled. "I want to work with my hands," he said stubbornly. So at the age of 14 he was apprenticed to an uncle who was a watchmaker. At 18 he decided to seek his fortune in America. He found work in a cousin's shop in Washington, D. C. There they made various instruments for the government and built models of inventions of all sorts that inventors brought to the Capitol to have patented.

The shop was moved to Baltimore in 1873, and it was there that Mergenthaler became interested in building a typesetting machine. One afternoon Charles T. Moore brought a contraption to the shop which he called a "stereotyping machine." "It has certain defects," he said, "and unless I can iron them out, my backers threaten to withdraw their support." Ottmar examined the machine. "I think we can fix it," he said confidently. In a few weeks he put it in shape, and

Moore's backers decided to go on with the invention.

The experience put a bee in the affable young German's bonnet: he decided to build a better typesetter. Moore's machine had used papier maché for the "matrix," on which the type was formed and the matrix itself was 40 lines long. The type was often blurred, almost illegible at times. Mergenthaler built one machine, another, and a third. But all were unsatisfactory. Then, the solution came to him — a metal line of type! His new machine would have matrices of single lines instead of the unwieldy 40, and he would make the matrices of brass instead of paper to make them stronger and to cast type that was uniformly legible. His fourth machine, completed in January of 1884, was a success. Basically his typesetter was a combination of four machines. It contained a typesetter keyboard for composition of copy, a magazine for storing the matrices, an attachment for casting type, and a mechanical system for returning the matrices to their proper place in the magazine.

The "linotype," as Mergenthaler's invention was called, is simple to operate, but actually it is a most intricate and complicated piece of machinery. The operator sits at the keyboard and types out the copy until a line is complete. Then he presses a lever and the matrices of the line are carried automatically to a position in front of a pot of molten type metal, a lead alloy, heated by a gas flame. Another lever is pressed and the liquid metal pours into the mold formed by the matrices. The metal cools to a solid almost instantly, and the line of type or "slug" is released automatically into a tray. In the meantime the matrices are lifted by a lever and redistributed in their proper places in the magazine.

The advantage of the linotype over the old method of setting type by hand can be easily understood. By the hand-set method, for instance, a compositor took an hour to set enough type for a book page, about 350 words. A linotype operator can set the same page in 8 minutes or less. The linotype is also economical, for it permits one man to do the work of seven or eight men using the old method. In fact, improvements in the linotype since Mergenthaler's death now permit the machine to set type without an operator. Rolls of tape with the words represented by a code of holes punched in it are run through the linotype, operating it automatically. One man can tend four to six machines operated by tapes.

Ottmar Mergenthaler became rich and famous through his invention, but he never ceased working on his machine, continually improving it. After Gutenberg's invention, Mergenthaler's linotype has done more to spread the printed word to the people of the world than any other invention in the field of printing.

RUDOLF CHRISTIAN KARL DIESEL

(1858–1913)

His Engine Provides Economical Power

THE principle on which an ice-making machine operated was indirectly responsible for the invention of the Diesel engine. Rudolf Diesel was attending the Institute of Technology in Munich, Germany when he first began thinking of a means to produce an engine which would provide more efficient and less expensive power. Steam engines were the prime movers of industry in the late 19th century, but their efficiency and the high cost of fuel to operate them left much to be desired.

A lecture on the inefficiency of the steam engine by one of his professors, Karl von Linde, led Diesel to study the merits and defects of the steam engine. Professor Linde also manufactured and operated ice-making machines, and, having taken a fancy to his brilliant young student, invited him to make a study of that machine as well. It was while undertaking this study that Diesel made an observation that was to be the basic principle for the engine he invented years later — that heat can generate power when it falls from a higher to a lower temperature.

Rudolf Diesel was born in Paris on March 18, 1858, of German parents. When he was 12 years old, his family moved to England, but Rudolf was sent to Germany for schooling. He was a brilliant student, and graduated from both trade school and college at the head of his class.

When he finished school in Munich, he got a job in Paris at one of the factories where Professor Linde's ice-making machines were made, later transferring to Berlin. Here he learned the practical side of engineering, and began tinkering with inventions of his own.

Trying to build an engine that would run more efficiently and economically, he first invented a steam engine that operated on ammonia gas. Then in 1892, Diesel invented the forerunner of his Diesel engine — an engine operating on the principle of internal combustion through self-ignition. He perfected the engine in 1897.

The idea had first come to him as a student when he watched the ice machine operate and observed that heat was converted to power to make ice. Diesel's engine was unique in that it mixed air and fuel (oil) inside the cylinder where the mixture was ignited by the heat of compression. The gasoline engine, by contrast, mixes the fuel and air before it enters the cylinder, where it is ignited by an electric spark. The difference gives the Diesel engine much more efficiency with less fuel consumption than the gasoline engine.

Rudolf Diesel's engines are used mainly to move heavy equipment such as trucks, trains, tractors, ships, and to operate power plants.

Rudolf Diesel did not live to see the full de-

velopment and wide application of his remarkable engine; in 1913 he fell overboard from a ship in the English channel and was drowned.

The applications of diesel power continue to expand even today. Because of its weight the diesel engine first found application in stationary installations such as power for factory machinery. Later diesel engines were installed in ships, and with the advent of electricity in powerhouses.

Some of these giant engines are as long as 80 feet and stand up to 35 feet high.

In many other applications diesel engines continue to replace steam and other power units. One of the most dramatic of these changes occurred only since World War II on the American railroads, where the conversion from steam to diesel power on major lines is now complete, Rudolf Diesel's engine having driven the iron horse from the rails.

GOTTLIEB DAIMLER

(1834-1900)

He Put the World on Wheels

IT IS close to midnight in the town of Cannstatt, Germany, back in the year 1883. A commissioner of police leading a squad of armed officers steals up to a villa at 13 Taubenheimstrasse. Inside the building, it has been reported, is a pair of counterfeiters hard at work making false coinage.

The police spring their trap. Guns drawn, they burst into the house.

Inside, the officers found two men hard at work — but they weren't making funny money. Operating in secret, Gottlieb Daimler and his friend and coworker Wilhelm Maybach were developing a new type of internal combustion engine — one of the ancestors of our automobile engines of today.

A great pioneer of automotive design, Gottlieb Daimler has been called, with much justice, the "father of the automobile." His motto, "Nothing But the Best," which hung framed in his workshop, guided him all through his lifetime, a lifetime dedicated to bringing the world forward into the motor age.

Daimler was born in the small town of Schorndorf, in Wurttemburg, on March 17th, 1834. This was a time when steam was the motive power of the world.

In 1807, a bare few decades before, "Fulton's Folly" had steamed majestically up the Hudson to open the hissing and sputtering era of steam transportation. Steamships, at the time of Daimler's birth, were plying the oceans, and he himself, in his youth, worked in the manufacture of steam locomotives.

When Gottlieb Daimler died, in 1900, the day of the gasoline engine, of the automobile, had arrived.

Gottlieb was the son of a baker, Johannes Daimler. But ovens and bread held no interest for this young man whose future lay in automotive engineering, a field which then did not even exist.

He was sent to the local public school, his father hoping that, as he was bright and had no interest in baking, he might become the town clerk. But Gottlieb was too bright to be taken in by that dreary prospect, either. Mechanics was his interest and nothing could stop him.

When he left school he was apprenticed to a gun-maker, that business being in a good condition due to the bad condition of Europe at the time. To complete his apprenticeship he designed and made a pair of beautifully wrought pistols, superbly crafted with technical perfection. The guns impressed his masters so that they tried to keep him with them. But the searching Daimler wanted to move on.

And so he did, going from trade to school to trade again, learning as much of the techniques of mechanics as he could absorb. And what he could absorb was considerable, as the world was finally to see.

Daimler's motorcycle was not graciously received by the local population. Neighbors laughed, police frowned, and the press proclaimed a danger to the entire community. "The gasoline is inflammable and the speed dangerous," they said. The machine was barred from the streets by the police who dutifully followed the lead of the press.

In secret, then, Daimler and Maybach installed an engine in a regular coach designed to be drawn by horses. With Maybach driving, the machine clattered around their back garden. The "horseless carriage" had arrived.

Daimler gave up motorcycles and automobiles for the time being and turned to making motorboats instead. The boat worked well, but the public again was frightened of the gasoline engines. The time Daimler employed a little subterfuge and decked his boat out with covered wire and porcelain insulators to give the impression that the vessel was electrically operated. This, somehow, made the local folk feel a little more secure.

Daimler's seventeen year old son, Paul, was of great help to his father and Maybach from around this time on. The men became busier and received many orders for their engines. The house on Taubenheimstrasse was no longer big enough for their needs. They moved to larger quarters and engaged a few employees.

The inventors continued their work, motorizing, among other things, the first streetcar and fire engine. Even aeronautical experiment was included in their efforts at that time.

They resumed their work on automobiles and developed a motorcar known as the "Steel-wheeler." This vehicle left the horse-carriage form behind. It was a two-seater of true automobile design.

At the Paris World's Fair of 1889 the Daimler-Maybach automobile was shown along with one exhibited by Karl Benz. Both vehicles were met by the public not with enthusiasm, but with distaste. But whether the public liked it or not, the automobile was here to stay.

In his work, Daimler developed the gear drive, left it, and returned to it. The gear drive is still the basic method of automotive operation today.

From 1857 to 1859 he studied engineering at the Polytechnic College in Stuttgart. He went to work in England, moved on to Belgium and France, and returned to Germany. There he worked his way up to foreman at one plant, then works director at another. Finally he moved up to an executive position in charge of development and manufacture.

During this time he met Emma Pauline Kurz, the lady who was to become his wife and mother of his five children.

Nikolaus August Otto, the inventor of the four-stroke gas engine, had established an engine factory at Dentz in 1872. Daimler went to work in the new factory as technical director. For ten years Daimler worked with Otto's company on the development of the internal-combustion engine. Working hard, without ever taking a holiday, Daimler often got up in the middle of the night in order to get back to his technical problems. He was a man who loved to work, and who had the physical stamina to maintain the pace he demanded of himself.

After ten years Daimler left Otto. He felt that he wanted to develop a smaller, more portable, and more powerful engine. As there was no interest in this project where he was, he broke his connection with Otto and persuaded his friend Maybach to come after him.

The two men went to work at the villa in Cannstatt—the one which was mistakenly raided by the police. Here the first Daimler engines were developed. Light and high-turning, they operated at 900 revolutions per minute. They weighed 88 pounds as against the Otto gas engines which weighed 725 pounds and turned over at a maximum of only 180 revolutions per minute.

The prototype of the automobile engine had arrived — but not the automobile as yet.

At this time, around 1885, Daimler and Maybach built the first motorbicycle ever devised. Around the same period a man named Karl Benz was experimenting with a three-wheeled motor vehicle. The firm of Karl Benz was later to be associated with Daimler's company in the manufacture of the now famous Mercedes-Benz automobile.

As Daimler persevered in his work, the automobile industry was born. In England, France, and the United States the manufacture of cars began. Despite difficulties with public acceptance and differences with business associates who were opposed to "wasting money" on experiments, Gottlieb Daimler kept moving forward.

Automobile racing began. Daimler's engines proved the value of the inventor's ideas of compact design and fast revolution, and Daimler himself did some racing.

But working, not racing, was the basis of this great inventor's life. And a full and productive life it was, rewarded by success and recognition in the end.

Less than a year before the inventor's death, he was honored by Emperor William II. The ruler asked to be shown the many kinds of Daimler vehicles. Tired and ill, Daimler sat with pride in front of his home as a parade of vehicles of all kinds drove by — buses, trucks, limousines, racing cars, and passenger vehicles.

Daimler died a few months later, on March 6, 1900. But the parade is still passing by — a parade of such great economic force that it forms a cornerstone of our American prosperity.

So we today, people of another country and another time, must look back to Gottlieb Daimler and his associates and acknowledge our debt to this giant of invention.

JOHN PHILIP HOLLAND

(1842–1914)

Man Travels Under the Sea

I<small>T WAS A</small> sunny day in March of 1898 and several fishermen were sitting patiently in their small boats in New York harbor, waiting for the fish to start biting. One in particular was sitting quietly in his boat, calmly puffing on his pipe and occasionally checking his lines, completely at peace in his private fisherman's world. The water rippled a short distance from his boat and what appeared to be a sea monster rose to the surface of the Hudson River for a few seconds, then disappeared as silently as it had come. The startled fisherman pulled in his lines and rowed to shore as fast as he could to tell the biggest fish story of his life.

But it was no sea monster that broke the waters of the Hudson that day — it was the father of the modern submarine, designed and built by John Philip Holland. On this trial run the *Holland*, as the underwater boat was called, was piloted by Captain Frank T. Cable, who often in later years related the story of the frightened fisherman. The little iron sub was to become a familiar sight in New York Harbor as it underwent more tests and trials, and the sea monster story was soon discounted.

But the *Holland* was not the first submarine to operate successfully. Other men before Holland had invented underwater boats, which, though crude, were successful. Perhaps the honor of building the first submarine should go to David Bushnell, who in 1775 built his *Turtle*

to operate in the same waters in an attempt to sink the British warship *Eagle* during the Revolutionary War. The *Turtle* was a success, but did little damage to the British fleet. Another pioneer submariner was Robert Fulton. He built a submarine for the French government during one of Napoleon's wars with England. His *Nautilus*, a hand-powered craft, was completed in 1801 and during her trials managed to sink an old schooner with a floating mine. Despite her success, Napoleon decided against using the *Nautilus* and Fulton gave up his ideas of building submarines, devoting himself to the invention of the steamboat.

During the American Civil War naval history was made when for the first time a submarine sank an enemy ship. The Confederate submarine *Hunley*, which was constructed partly from an old iron boiler, torpedoed and sank the Union warship *Housatonic* in the harbor of Charleston, South Carolina. The *Hunley* and her entire crew were lost in the engagement, but the world was finally awakened to the role the submarine could play in future wars. It was almost 35 years later, however, before the submarine was accepted by the navies of the world. John Holland's was the first. During the time he was building his submarines another American, Simon Lake, also designed and built several successful submarines, but Holland's design was the most accepted and he is generally considered the inventor of the submarine.

John Philip Holland was a school teacher in Ireland before he migrated to the United States in 1873. He continued his career as a teacher in the United States, but his interest, aroused by the sinking of the *Housatonic* and by reading

He built several boats with varying degrees of success before the *Holland* was launched in 1898. By 1900 the United States Navy had accepted its first Holland-designed submarine. The first *Holland* was almost a midget compared to the giant submarines plying the depths of the

Jules Verne's *Twenty Thousand Leagues Under The Sea*, turned more and more toward the building of an underwater boat. His first plans for a submarine were drawn in the hospital while recuperating from a broken leg. On his recovery Holland began his career as a submarine builder.

seas today. It was a cigar-shaped craft with a small turret or conning tower projecting about 18 inches above the deck. The boat was 53 feet long, ten feet in diameter, and weighed 73 tons. She used a gasoline engine when running on the surface and electric batteries when submerged, and could travel at speeds of seven and five knots respectively. Her cruising range was 1,500 miles on the surface and about 40 miles under water. The *Holland* was armed with a torpedo tube for firing one of the newly invented Whitehead torpedoes. She had to surface to aim when she launched her "fish" because at that time the periscope had not been invented.

Holland, with other men, formed the Electric Boat Company, which is still building submarines for the United States Navy. After the acceptance of the first *Holland* in 1900, they built many submarines for the United States Navy as well as selling their boats to England, Russia, and Japan. The Holland design remained the standard for most submarines built during World Wars I and II, with improvements by others making it one of the most deadly weapons man has ever devised.

The only real major change in submarines since the first *Holland* came in 1955 when the first atomic submarine, the *Nautilus*, was launched. Nuclear powered submarines can cruise around the world without surfacing — a far cry from the 40 miles the little *Holland* was able to travel under water. But even the nuclear-powered submarines owe much to the basic designs of the father of the submarine — John Philip Holland.

GUGLIELMO MARCONI

(1874–1937)

Wireless Telegraphy Spans the Ocean

THE basis for our modern system of communication was laid in the early 19th century with the invention of the telegraph by Samuel Morse and the telephone by Alexander Graham Bell. But perhaps the greatest contribution in this field was the invention of wireless telegraphy by a young Italian inventor, Guglielmo Marconi. His invention led to the development of radio and television, and was responsible in great part for the many benefits the vast communication systems of the world offer man today.

Marconi, who was born in Bologna, Italy on April 25, 1874, never attended public school. He was from a wealthy family, and various tutors were responsible for his formal education. Marconi's father maintained a large scientific library in their home, and Guglielmo showed an early interest in electricity, chemistry, and the use of steam. He learned the Morse code at an early age, and in his home made crude experiments with electricity, including those Benjamin Franklin had introduced.

But what really excited his imagination as a boy and evoked the idea of the wireless telegraph was an article he came upon written by the scientist Heinrich Rudolph Hertz, the discoverer of Hertzian waves. Hertz related how during one of his experiments tiny sparks occurred in the gap of a loop of wire at one end of the room when he radiated electro-magnetic waves with an electric oscillator at the other end

of the room. What impressed Hertz, and Marconi, was that the two instruments had not been connected by a conductor. The current creating the sparks had flowed through the air. Could a telegraph be made to work by this system, Marconi wondered.

The youth plunged into a study of all that had been learned of electricity at that time, reading the works of such men as Faraday, Edouard Branley, Sir Oliver Lodge, and others. Using their contributions and experiments, he soon built an exciter and coherer (a crude receiver) in his attic laboratory. Using this apparatus he managed to make a bell ring 30 feet away without being attached to the exciter by wires. With this success under his belt, he constructed his first wireless telegraph. His transmitter was a Morse telegraph key hooked to a spark coil powered by batteries, and a ground and aerial. His receiver was a crude detector hooked to a Morse telegraph sounder, also powered with batteries, and another ground and aerial. At the age of 20 Guglielmo Marconi sent his first wireless signal (the letter "S" in Morse code) a distance of 200 feet.

Marconi's indulgent father was much impressed by his son's accomplishment, and tried to interest the Italian government in the invention, but to no avail. The determined young Marconi went to England, where he obtained a patent for his wireless telegraph in February of 1896.

Through the good offices of the English Post Office Department, he demonstrated in 1897 on the Salisbury Plains that he could send a signal over a distance of nine miles. In 1899 he sent a message across the English Channel to France. He was invited to Italy to make ship to shore experiments, but returned to England soon after to form the Wireless Telegraph and Signal Company, Ltd., later known as the Marconi Wireless Telegraph Company. The new company built instruments which were first used on light ships and light houses to announce the arrival of ocean going ships, but soon the system was used on ships at sea for navigation and safety purposes.

With the company a success and money no object, Marconi decided to see if his wireless telegraph could span the ocean. He built a 25,000 watt station at Poldhu in Cornwall, and then traveled to St. John's in Newfoundland to try the experiment. On December 14, 1901, the first signal, again the letter "S" in Morse code, traveled through the air some 1,800 miles across the Atlantic. There were still many "bugs" to be worked out of the system, but in 1905 Marconi managed to send a signal from Poldhu to a station on Cape Cod in the United States, a distance of some 3,000 miles.

By 1907 this young Italian inventor, then a mere 33 years old, established regular transatlantic wireless telegraphy communication. Marconi expanded his company to a worldwide

wireless communication system, and worked to improve wireless for ships at sea, invented a direction finder to aid in navigation, and experimented with using short waves in his system instead of long waves.

His invention sparked the beginning of the electronic age. Wireless telephone was developed in the United States by Professor Reginald Fessendom as early as 1901. Radio began to take its first baby steps as Flemming used the principle of the "Edison effect" to develop a detector tube with a filament and plate, with Lee de Forest adding a grid as the third element shortly thereafter to make radio possible. And these, in turn, led to the development of the first television in the 1920's.

But Guglielmo Marconi laid the groundwork for all the systems of wireless communication we have today, and the young Italian inventor who built the first wireless telegraph at the age of 20 must surely be listed on the rolls of those we call "Giants of Invention."

WILBUR WRIGHT

(1867–1912)

ORVILLE WRIGHT

(1871–1948)

Man Learns to Fly

EVERYTHING was ready. The white-winged flying machine was on its launching rails and the twin propellers whirred as the tiny motor was warmed up before take-off. Would it fly? In a moment they would know. The three other men present held their breath as Orville Wright climbed aboard the fragile craft and signalled that he was ready to go. With his brother Wilbur running alongside to steady the wings, this pioneer pilot guided the flying machine along its wooden launching tracks. For 40 feet the airplane clung to the wooden rails, then with a sudden lurch it was airborne. For the first time in history man had flown in a heavier-than-air machine!

That first flight at Kitty Hawk, North Caroline, on December 17, 1903, lasted for only 12 seconds and covered a distance of 120 feet. But despite the brevity of the flight, it marked the first time a man had ever flown in a powered aircraft, and the age of aviation was born. The fathers of this new era were a pair of bicycle makers from Dayton, Ohio — Wilbur and Orville Wright.

The Wright brothers were very close, and worked as a team both in their business ventures and in their efforts to learn to fly. Their first business was a weekly newspaper. The ingenious Orville actually built the press they used. Later they gave up the newspaper and concentrated on job printing. In 1893 they opened their bi-

cycle shop. The shop was a success and as business grew they expanded from a repair shop to the manufacture of their own brand of bikes which they assembled from purchased parts. The profits from this business financed their experiments in flight.

As boys the Wright brothers had flown kites and built their own version of a toy helicopter their father had given them, but it was not until 1896 that they became interested in building a "flying machine." It was a newspaper story of the death of Otto Lilienthal, one of aviation's early pioneers who died when one of his experimental gliders crashed, that aroused their interest in flying. They decided to build a machine themselves.

They went about their task in their usual methodical way, first reading and studying everything that had been published on the subject up to that time. Needless to say, there was little to go on. Man had been trying to fly since Leonardo da Vinci's first experiments in the 15th century. Early pioneers in this field included Sir George Cayley, who described plans for a flying machine in 1809; the German Lilienthal, who started his glider experiments in 1871; and Percy S. Pilcher, who like Lilienthal was killed while flying in one of his "kites." Others included Professor Samuel P. Langley, who flew a model airplane powered by steam in 1903, and Octave Chanute, who gave the Wright brothers the benefit of his experience in gliders and other flying experiments.

After completing their study of the subject, the Wrights decided their first flying machine would be a two-winged glider. They built the craft and took it to Kitty Hawk, North Carolina for testing because of the favorable prevailing winds in that area. By October of 1900 they were ready. The first glider had no tail, but had an elevator projecting in front of the craft. Lateral control was achieved by movements of the pilot's body as he lay prone on the bottom wing. The white-winged glider had a wing span of 18 feet, and proved a success. They returned to Kitty Hawk in 1901 and again in 1902 with larger, improved gliders, which by now were equipped with tails to aid stability. After the 1902 experiments they decided that they knew enough about controlling and flying an airplane to attempt to build a powered flying machine.

For power they decided to use an internal combustion engine instead of steam because of the saving in weight it would afford. They were unable to find a manufacturer who would build one to their specifications, and decided to build their own. Despite the fact that they had never before built an engine, the ingenious bicycle makers built a four-cylinder motor in their shop in Dayton that produced 12 horsepower and was still light enough to be used in an aircraft. They stuck to their biplane design, which incorporated all the features of their latest glider — the elevator in front and a tail. The little motor was powered to chain-driven, pusher type, propellers.

After the historic first flight on December 17, 1903, the Wright brothers made two more trips in their white-winged craft that day before a sudden gust of wind wrecked the machine. The longest flight that year covered a distance of 852 feet in 57 seconds.

Their achievements were generally scoffed at,

but in 1904 they were back in the air again, determined to show the world that man could fly. Their flights at Simms Station near Dayton showed much improvement in their flying machine. They managed to stay aloft for several minutes at a time and one flight actually covered a distance of nine miles. They were truly pioneers, for they had to teach themselves how to fly. No one could tell them how to bank a plane or how to control their crude machine when it went into a stall. Using this experience they built a bigger plane in 1905 with better controls. This craft managed to attain a speed of 38 miles an hour, and flights of 24 miles became commonplace for the two bicycle makers.

There were still many doubting Thomases, but the Wrights persevered. In 1908 Wilbur took one of their planes to France, and his exhibitions with the "flying machine" there made him a national hero on the scale of Lindbergh who captured the hearts of the French some 20 years later. By now the planes the Wrights were building could stay in the air for several hours and cover two to three hundred miles. The pilot sat upright, and a passenger could be carried.

After 1908 their success was assured. They sold the French rights to their invention for $100,000 and the Italian rights went for $200,000. Their planes sold all over Europe, and in 1909 the United States government got into the act and purchased one of their planes for the army at a cost of $30,000. Their airplane factory in Dayton prospered, and the two brothers were lionized wherever they went. Wilbur died in 1912, but Orville continued his interest in aviation, contributing to the era he and his brother had inaugurated on the sandy beach of Kitty Hawk in 1903 until his death in 1948.

LEE DE FOREST

(1873–1961)

The Human Voice Conquers Space

Radio was made possible by the simple innovation of adding a piece of twisted platinum wire to one of Thomas Edison's incandescent lamps. Until this discovery by Lee De Forest in 1907, the only means of transmitting the human voice was by telephone. Marconi's wireless, although able to span oceans, could only transmit the dots and dashes of the Morse code. De Forest's simple invention not only made radio possible, but also gave birth to the entire electronics industry.

As a youth De Forest spent much of his time trying to invent the products of his fertile imagination—a perpetual motion machine, a "talking device," and others. Most of these youthful attempts at invention were impractical, but they served to influence De Forest to study electricity in college rather than follow in the footsteps of his father, who was a minister.

Upon graduation from Yale University, De Forest went to work for the Western Electric Company in Chicago where he was employed at the task of wiring telephone switchboards. While a student at Yale he had become interested in Marconi's newly invented wonder of wireless telegraphy. Despite the fact that little was known of the wireless in America, De Forest determined to improve upon Marconi's invention.

Using the company's laboratory during his lunch period and after-hours to conduct his experiments, De Forest invented a detector he called a "sponder" which was far superior to Marconi's. He formed the American De Forest Wireless Company, and large contracts from the Army and Navy for his wireless sets made the company an immediate success. However, while traveling in Europe to demonstrate his invention, his associates gained control of the company and of De Forest's patents, and forced him out of the firm, leaving him almost penniless.

The only thing his ruthless associates did not strip him of were his rough plans for the radio vacuum tube. They thought it worthless. However, once again the inventor's talent rescued him, and in 1907 he perfected the tube. Radio and the electronic industry were born. While trying to find a still better detector, De Forest investigated the possibilities of adapting Edison's incandescent lamp to his purposes. He knew of the phenomenon called the "Edison effect," whereby when the plate in the lamp was charged positively, a stream of electrons flowed across the gap between the plate and the filament of the lamp to set up a circuit when the plate in the lamp was charged positively. De Forest reasoned that Edison's lamp and this peculiar "effect" might be used to generate waves of any desired length and thus be used as a detector.

After much experimenting he managed to control the flow of current with his twisted wire (grid) placed between the plate and filament of the lamp. At first De Forest used his three-electrode vacuum tube, or "audion," as he called his invention, as a detector only. It was not until some five years after its invention that he realized it could also be used as an amplifier of sound.

The development of radio was slow, but, once the vacuum tube was invented, sure. As early as 1906 De Forest, while still experimenting with his "audion," was able to transmit the human voice for short distances. By 1909 he was broadcasting music a distance of several blocks. On January 20, 1910, he broadcast the operas *Pagliacci* and *Cavalleria Rusticana* from the stage of the Metropolitan Opera House in New York. Audiences in three locations throughout the city heard Enrico Caruso sing the starring roles in this historical broadcast.

But despite these early successes, radio didn't catch the public fancy. For years De Forest was the only broadcaster in the country, his only supporters a handful of "hams" (amateur radio operators) who were intrigued by the magic of radio.

When radio finally was developed about 1920, De Forest found himself once again out in the cold. Financial difficulties had forced him to sell his patents for $50,000, and others gained the fame and fortune that was rightly his as the inventor of the magic tube that fathered radio, radar, television, and other marvels of the electronic age.

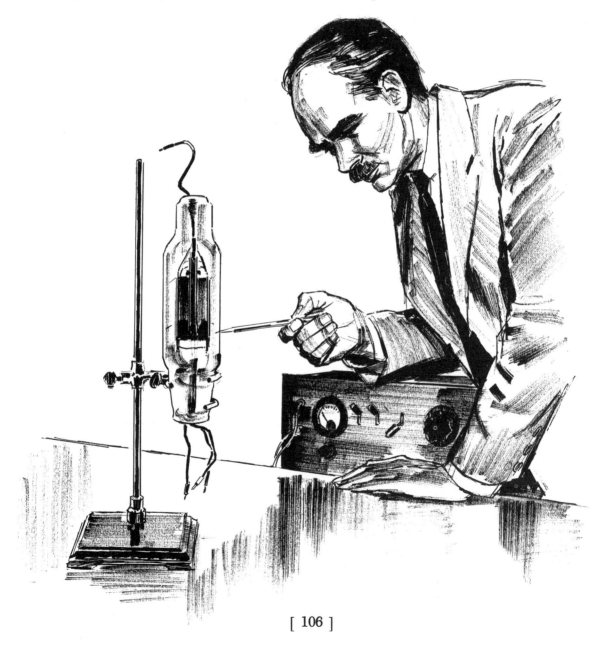

ROBERT H. GODDARD

(1882–1945)

The Beginning of the Space Age

THE three men carefully lifted the 10-foot "bird" onto the portable launcher, made some adjustments on it, then stepped back to view their work for a minute. It was quiet and peaceful in the field on the farm near Auburn, Massachusetts; so tranquil that one might think that no other world but this existed. But the event about to transpire was to shatter any such thoughts and give man the means to probe the mysteries and worlds which might exist in space.

While his wife readied her camera to record the take-off, Dr. Robert H. Goddard opened the propellent valves on the rocket and an assistant ignited the rocket's motor with a blow torch attached to the end of a long pole. With a roar the rocket took off from the launcher and the little "bird" flew for two and a half seconds — the first liquid-propelled rocket ever launched. This historic date, March 16, 1926, not only marked the invention of the liquid-fueled rocket by Dr. Goddard, but it also ushered in the Space Age.

Although Goddard is recognized as the father of modern rocketry and the inventor of the liquid-propelled rocket, he was not the first to invent a rocket. That honor goes to an unknown Chinese inventor who, around A.D. 1230, built rockets powered with gunpowder to repel the invading Mongols. Since that time man has used rockets as weapons of war or as signalling devices, improving them from time to time, but always clinging to the method of using solid fuel (usually gunpowder) as the propellent. It was Goddard, however, who adapted liquid fuel as a means of propulsion to make it not only one of the most formidable weapons of all time, but also a most sophisticated scientific instrument for man's exploration of space.

Goddard began his work with rockets in 1909. By that time he had already developed the idea of multiple rockets and in theory had worked out plans for using hydrogen and oxygen as fuel for rockets in interplanetary flights. At this time, in fact up until the 1930's, anyone considering a "shot at the moon" or any other type of rocket probe into space was considered a lunatic or crackpot. Goddard, who was a professor at Clark University in Worcester, Massachusetts, had to carry out his work in secrecy to avoid ridicule. He persevered in his experiments, however, working mostly in his spare time and with insufficient funds. Finally the Smithsonian Institute and later the United States Army became interested in his work and granted him financial aid. Working for the Army during World I, he developed a long range bombardment rocket and an early version of the bazooka, but the war ended before either could be used. After the war he continued his experiments, but concentrated his efforts on developing a liquid instead of solid fuel to propel his rockets. His

long years of labor bore fruit with the historic launching in March of 1926.

The first liquid fuel used was a mixture of liquid oxygen and gasoline fed into the motor from separate tanks. The tanks were located at the rear of the first rocket, but in subsequent models Goddard set the pattern which is now standard and put the motor at the rear of the rocket. The first ignition system was about as crude as it was simple — the propellent valves were opened by hand and a blowtorch applied. After this initial success Goddard continued his experiments, moving his laboratory to Roswell, New Mexico, near what is now the White Sands proving grounds. With financial aid supplied in great part by the Guggenheim Foundation, his rockets grew in size and sophistication. During the 1930's he developed most of the basic ideas incorporated in the rockets and guided missiles in use today such as propellent pumps, gyro-controls, instrumentation, and many others. Even the V-2 rockets used by the Germans in World War II were based on Goddard's pioneer efforts.

As early as 1919, in a treatise entitled *A Method of Reaching Extreme Altitudes*, Goddard proposed trying to reach the moon by rocket. He didn't live to see ideas of space flight carried out, but every time a "Jupiter" or "Atlas" roars off its launching pad to send a man into space or a satellite into orbit, Goddard's ideas and inventions go along with it.

LEO HENDRIK BAEKELAND

(1863–1944)

Plastics Revolutionize Industry

THE SEARCH for a substitute for shellac led to the invention of Bakelite — the plastic that revolutionized most of the industries of the world. Leo Baekeland had already made a fortune through his invention of Velox photographic paper, and at 35 retired to live on his estate in Yonkers, New York, on the banks of the Hudson River. But the inventive urge was strong in this Belgian-born American and rather than rest on laurels won in the field of photography, he turned his talents to the field of chemistry.

Leo Hendrick Baekeland was born in Ghent, Belgium. He showed an interest in photography and chemistry at an early age. Upon graduation from the University of Ghent Baekeland became a science instructor at the school, but, while traveling in the United States, was persuaded to settle here. He invented Velox paper, and his fortune was made. The Eastman Kodak Company bought his firm for one million dollars.

Despairing of the idleness of retirement at the age of 35, Baekeland turned one of the buildings on his Yonkers estate into a laboratory and began his research to find a substitute for shellac. Studying the experiments of other chemists in the field before him, particularly Adolph Bayer, he found that phenols and aldehydes when combined with heat left a hard, porous substance that could not be dissolved.

It was obvious that this material would be valuable if it could be controlled. Baekeland set out to accomplish this. Other chemists had said that the application of too much heat would make control of the substance impossible, but on a hunch Baekeland decided that more, not less, heat was needed for effective control. He tried his theory, and found that by baking a mixture of phenol and formaldehyde with alkalies added in an oven of compressed air at high temperatures, he could control the substance. The product he took from his oven was light, tough, indissoluble, and would resist heat, acids, and electricity. His invention was perfected in 1906.

Bakelite, as the inventor called his new plastic, was used for almost everything. It practically revolutionized the electrical industry, became indispensable in the manufacture of autos and radios, and was used to make everything from telephones to billiard balls.

JOHN LOGIE BAIRD

(1888–1946)

The Magic Screen of Television

The first star of television was a ventriloquist's dummy. The show was staged in an attic studio in London, England, on October 2, 1926. The image of the dummy that showed up on the screen of the crude television receiver was the first true television picture ever telecast.

John Logie Baird had been experimenting for only two years when he managed to transmit a face that was recognizable on the screen. He was alone in his two-room attic workshop when the miracle occurred. The receiver was in one room, the transmitter with the dummy before it in the other. He was so elated by his success that he rushed downstairs, dragged an office boy from the floor below to his laboratory, and placed him before the camera. Racing into the other room he gazed at the screen, and sure cnough, the image of the office boy was plain.

Baird, who was born in Helensburgh, Scotland, on August 13, 1888, had retired from business in 1922 because of ill health. His business ventures ranged from selling socks to running a jam and preserve factory in Trinidad; later he sold soap in London. But his health broke down, and at the age of 34, with nothing else to do, he began to tinker with television. Others were also working in the field, including Charles Jenkins, Vladmir Zworykins, and Philo Farnsworth, but none had as yet succeeded in telecasting a true image. All of these pioneers were indebted to the earlier work and discoveries of Paul Nipflow, Thomas Edison, Heinrich Hertz, John Fleming, and Lee De Forest.

Baird, working with home-made equipment, managed in 1925 to transmit "shadow graphs," but not clear images. His theory was simple enough. When a face is televised, the variations of light from the features are transmitted by photoelectric cells into variations of electric current, which modulate a radio wave. This wave travels through space to the receiver, where it is retranslated into electric signals. These signals direct the light that forms the original image on the screen.

Baird's television used a powerful beam of light to scan the face and then transmit the image point by point. The receiver would reassemble the face in the reverse of this procedure. His trouble was in finding a suitable photoelectric cell. He could transmit shadows, but not faces. He tried everything, even a human eye, as a light-sensitive cell. Nothing worked until his experiment with the dummy.

He gave public demonstration of his TV in 1926, and in 1927 succeeded in transmitting pictures from Jordan to Glasgow, a distance of 400 miles. In 1928 he telecast a picture across the Atlantic, and in 1931 caught the imagination of the English public by televising the Derby, Britain's leading racing event. By 1936 regular broadcasts were being made by the British Broadcasting Corporation, and TV sets were available to the public. TV also caught on in the United States, but it was not until 1939 that regular broadcasts were being made.

Today, television is as common a sight in the home as the telephone or electric lights. Millions of sets, both black and white and color, are built each year, and the TV industry has grown into a multi-billion dollar enterprise. And much of this miracle is due to a Scotsman who had to retire because of ill health.

SIR FRANK WHITTLE

(1907–   )

Airplanes Fly Without Propellers

THE test pilot climbed into the cockpit of the odd-looking aircraft and "lighted the torch." To some of the spectators present that day in May of 1941 it seemed strange, almost foolhardy, for a man to attempt to fly a plane that had no propeller. Not so Frank Whittle; he knew the turbo-jet engine he had designed to power the experimental Gloster E-28 would not only work successfully but would eventually revolutionize the aviation industry.

On that historic flight from the Cranwell Air Base in England the turbo-jet propelled E-28 flew for 17 minutes and attained a speed of 370 miles per hour. This was far faster than the speed of the piston-engine-powered *Spitfires* with which the Royal Air Force was so successfully winning the "Battle of Britain" over London and the English Channel. It is true that the Germans had flown a jet powered airplane some two years earlier, but their engine design was inspired by the publication in 1932 of Whittle's turbo-jet patent.

Whittle's successful flight in 1941 terminated his 13 years of intense effort and frustration to make jet propulsion a reality. The idea came to him as he was finishing his air cadet training at Cranwell in 1928. The Royal Air Force required the cadets to write a thesis on some scientific subject prior to graduation. Whittle predicted in an article called "The Future Developments in Aircraft Design" that planes of the future would fly at high altitudes and at speeds of 500 miles per hour or better. This led him to the conclusion that conventional piston engines would not be sufficient for the purpose and he began to think about how to design an engine to do the job.

It was while serving as a fighter pilot that he got the idea for his turbo-jet. The principle for using a gas turbine for compressing air to drive the propeller was already known. Whittle's idea was to use the exhaust from the compressor turbine as a jet for propelling the airplane, doing away with the propellor altogether. By 1930 he had the plans and specifications drawn up and in 1931 was granted a patent for his turbo-jet engine. But it took six long years before Whittle saw his first engine built. Private industry and the government were not interested at the time, and Whittle had to go it alone as best he could on a flight officer's pay.

Realizing he needed more technical knowledge, he persuaded the Air Ministry in 1934 to send him to Cambridge to obtain a degree in engineering. In 1936, with the approval of the Royal Air Force, he formed a company with civilian backing to build an experimental turbo-jet engine. With little money and much ingenuity the company managed to turn out an engine by April of 1937. It ran all right, but it took four more years to iron out the bugs before they had an engine that would fly.

Whittle's turbo-jet was simply a device for producing a powerful jet of hot gases from the rear of the plane to propel it. Essentially it is a large, horizontal pipe into which air is sucked at the front end, compressed and blown out as hot gases at the rear. The moving parts are very simple — basically a single shaft with a fan at the front and a turbine at the rear. The problems to be solved to make the engine practicable were threefold: to build a compressor more powerful than any then in existence; to construct chambers for burning the compressed air and fuel which would resist the intense heat built up; and to find a metal for the turbine blades which would stand up.

Whittle and his associates solved these problems, but it was not until 1941 that they had an engine that would fly. It took several more years for the turbo-jet engine to come into its own. But when it did it almost completely revolutionized the aviation industry. Whittle, who had signed over the rights to his engine to the British government, retired from the Royal Air Force as an air commodore in 1948. Later in the year he was knighted, and the grateful government awarded him a grant of 100,000 pounds for his invention. Jets are so common nowadays that no one ever stops to wonder what ever happened to the propeller. If they did the answer could be simply Frank Whittle.

MAJOR INVENTIONS

Date	Invention	Inventor	Country
c. 250 B.C.	Water screw	Archimedes	Greek
c. 161 B.C.	Quadrant	Hipparchus	Greek
c. 50 B.C.	Water wheel with gears	Vitruvius	Roman
c. 25 B.C.	Screw presses	Vitruvius	Roman
c. 66 A.D.	Dioptra (surveyors)	Hero of Alexandria	Roman
1450	Adjustable type mold (printing press)	Johann Gutenberg	Germany
c. 1496	Power driven spindle	Leonardo da Vinci	Italian
c. 1496	Rolling mill	Leonardo da Vinci	Italian
c. 1496	Screw cutting lathe	Leonardo da Vinci	Italian
1589	Knitting machine	William Lee	England
1590	Compound microscope	Zacharius Jansen	Dutch
1593	Thermometer	Galileo Galilei	Italian
1609	Refracting telescope	Galileo Galilei	Italian
1620	Screw printing press	William J. Blaeu	Dutch
1630	Astronomical telescope (Keplers)	Christopher Schriener	German
1636	Micrometer	William Gascoigne	English
1642	Adding machine	Blaise Pascal	French
1643	Barometer	Evangelista Torricelli	Italian
1654	Air pump	Otto Von Guericke	German
1656	Pendulum clock	Christian Huygens	Dutch
1668	Reflecting telescope	Sir Isaac Newton	England
1671	Multiplying machine	G. W. Von Leibnitz	German
1690	First steam engine (using a piston)	Denis Papin	French
1700	Steam propelled three-wheeled carriage	Richard Argnot	French
1709	Coke burning iron furnace	Abraham Darby	England
1714	Typewriter	Henry Mill	England
1714	Mercury thermometer	G. D. Fahrenheit	German
1717	Diving bell	Edmund Halley	England
1725	Stereotyping	William Ged	Scotland
1740	Steel crucible process	Robert Huntsman	England
1746	Leyden jar	John Bevis	England
1749	Chronometer	John Harrison	England
1754	Heliometer	John Dolland	England
1756	Achromatic lens	John Dolland	England
1760	Lightning rod	Benjamin Franklin	United States
1764	Spinning jenny	James Hargreaves	England
1765	Steam engine (condensing)	James Watt	Scotland
1769	Throttle spinning	Richard Arkwright	England
1769	Steam engine perfected	James Watt	Scotland
1776	First U. S. submarine	David Bushnell	United States
1777	Circular wood saw	Samuel Miller	England
1779	Spinning jenny improved	Samuel Compton	England
1780	Bifocal lens	Benjamin Franklin	United States
1783	Gas balloon	J. E. and E. M. Montgolfier	French
1784	Cast iron plow	James Small	Scotland
1785	Power loom	Edmund Cartwright	England

| --- | --- | --- | --- |
1785	Parachute	Francois Blanchard	French
1786	Threshing machine	Andrew Meikle	Scotland
1786	First U. S. steamboat	John Fitch	United States
1793	Cotton gin	Eli Whitney	United States
1795	Hydraulic press	Joseph Bramah	England
1796	Lithography	Aloys Senefelder	German
1796	Cast iron plow improved	Charles Newbold	United States
1800	Electric battery	Alessandro Volta	Italian
1804	Rocket	Sir William Congreve	England
1804	Food canning process	Nicolas Appert	French
1805	Electroplating process	Luigi Brugnatelli	Italian
1807	Steamboat	Robert Fulton	United States
1808	Electric arc light	Sir Humphry Davy	England
1810	Breech loading rifle	John M. Hall	United States
1811	Steam printing press	Friedrich Konig	German
1812	Storage battery	J. B. Ritter	German
1814	Steam locomotive	George Stephenson	England
1815	Stethoscope	Rene Laennec	French
1819	Modern cast iron plow	Jethro Wood	United States
1819	Galvanometer	J. S. Schweigger	German
1820	Calculating machine	Charles Babbage	England
1822	Multicolored printing	Peter Force	United States
1822	Platen printing press	Daniel Treatwell	United States
1822	Typesetter	William Church	United States
1824	Portland cement	Joseph Aspdin	United States
1825	Improved steam locomotive	George Stephenson	England
1825	Electromagnet	William Sturgeon	England
1828	Hot air blast furnace	J. B. Neilson	Scotland
1830	Sewing machine	B. Thimonnies	French
1831	Flanged railroad rail	Robert L. Stevens	United States
1833	Reaper	Cyrus H. McCormick	United States
1835	Revolver	Samuel Colt	United States
1836	Telegraph	Samuel F. B. Morse	United States
1838	Steam hammer	James Nasmyth	Scotland
1837	Photography	Louis Daguerre	French
1844	Vulcanized rubber	Charles Goodyear	United States
1845	Pneumatic tire	Robert W. Thompson	England
1846	Sewing machine improved	Elias Howe	United States
1846	Guncotton	C. F. Schonbein	Germany
1847	Rotary printing press	Richard H. Hoe	United States
1850	Electric locomotive	Charles G. Page	United States
1851	Refrigerating machine	John Gorrie	United States
1852	Gyroscope	Jean Foncault	French
1852	Airship	Henri Giffard	French
1853	Condensed milk	Gail Borden	United States
1853	Electrolysis process	Michael Farraday	England
1855	Safety matches	J. E. Lundstrom	Sweden
1855	Bunsen burner	Robert W. Bunsen	Germany
1856	Bessemer steel process	Sir Henry Bessemer	England
1858	Refrigerator	Ferdinand Carre	French
1858	Cable car	E. A. Gardner	United States
1859	Gas engine	Jean Lenoir	French
1860	First electric lamp	Joseph W. Swan	England
1861	Steam elevator	Elisha G. Otis	United States
1861	Motion picture projector	Coleman Sellers	United States
1862	Gatling gun	Richard J. Gatling	United States

Date	Invention	Inventor	Country
1864	Pullman sleeping car	George M. Pullman	United States
1865	Bicycle	Pierre Lallement	French
1866	Dynamite	Alfred B. Noble	Sweden
1866	Open hearth steel process	Sir William Siemens	England
1866	Self-propelled torpedo	Robert Whitehead	England
1869	Railway air brake	George Westinghouse	United States
1873	Quadruplex telegraph	Thomas A. Edison	United States
1876	Telephone	Alexander G. Bell	United States
1876	Four-cycle gas engine	Nikolaus A. Otto	German
1877	Glider	Otto Lillienthal	German
1877	Phonograph	Thomas A. Edison	United States
1879	Cathode ray tube	Sir William Crookes	England
1879	Cash register	James Ritty	United States
1879	Incandescent lamp	Thomas A. Edison	United States
1881	Color photography	Frederick E. Ives	United States
1884	Motor car	F. A. J. Loffler	German
1884	Fountain pen	Lewis E. Waterman	United States
1884	Linotype	Ottmar Mergenthaler	United States
1885	Automobile	Gottlieb Daimler	German
1888	Kodak camera	George Eastman	United States
1892	Diesel engine	Rudolf Diesel	German
1892	A.C. electric motor	Nikola Tesla	United States
1895	Photoelectric cell	Julius Elster	German
1895	Wireless telegraphy	Guglielmo Marconi	Italian
1895	First successful submarine	John P. Holland	United States
1900	Caterpillar tractor	Benjamin Holt	United States
1900	Rigid airship	Ferdinand Von Zepplin	German
1903	Airplane	Wright brothers	United States
1904	Practical electron tube	Sir John Fleming	England
1904	First photo transmitted by wireless	Arthur Korn	German
1905	Gyroscopic compass	Elmer A. Sperry	United States
1907	Radio vacuum tube	Lee De Forest	United States
1907	Plastics	Leo H. Baekeland	United States
1911	Air conditioning	Willis H. Carrier	United States
1911	Hydroplane	Glenn H. Curtis	United States
1913	Radio receivers	R. A. Fessenden	Canada
		Ernst Alexandenos	United States
1913	Talking motion pictures	Thomas A. Edison	United States
1913	Geiger counter	Hans Geiger	German
1913	Ramjet engine	Rene Lorin	French
1914	Improved radio transmitter	Ernst Alexanderson	United States
1916	X-ray tube	William D. Coolidge	United States
1925	Television	John L. Baird	Scotland
		Charles F. Jenkins	United States
1926	First liquid propelled rocket	R. W. Goddard	United States
1928	Autogiro	Juan de la Cierva	Spain
1931	Cyclotron	Ernest O. Lawrence	United States
1932	Pulse jet engine	Paul Schmidt	German
1935	Radar	Sir Robert Watt	Scotland
1939	Helicopter	Igor Sikorski	United States
1945	Atom bomb	U. S. scientists	
1952	Hydrogen bomb	U. S. scientists	
1957	First man-made satellite	Russian scientists	
1962	Tiros (first weather satellite)	U. S. scientists	
1962	Telestar (first television satellite)	U. S. scientists and industry	